THE RECIPE

LIVING LIFE WITH EASE

RAMDAS ORMOND

 Bhakti Books, LLC

ISBN-13: 979-8-9892836-0-6 (Paperback edition)

ISBN-13: 979-8-9892836-1-3 (Ebook edition)

PRAISE FOR THE RECIPE

The Recipe is filled with easy to use, easy to remember tips to help distinguish between what can be changed and what must be accepted. If the reflections in the book are used, life can be less crazy, more aware and content.

— SITA K.

I integrate the recipe seamlessly into my everyday life when I face resistance to any situation. Recently, on a difficult travel day, I locked my keys in the car. The recipe prompted me to say, "This is like this", and I immediately began investigating and following Ramdas' instructions. I sailed through the whole experience with grace. The Recipe kept me calm, centered and able to engage open heartedly.

— SUZANNE C.

Ramdas Ormond is a heart-centered teacher who uses The Recipe to incorporate ancient teachings in a simple, accessible, and transformative way, accessible to all.

— INDU A.

The Recipe is more than self-help, more than philosophy and more than a memoir. It is all three combined into a book you will want to have within reach for years to come. You'll find yourself using its easy steps to solve any and all problems you come across in life. For me, it has simplified my responses to everything from a precocious preschooler to the purchase of an electric vehicle. It works for every time, place, age, or gender.

— MYRA R.

Dedicated

To You

CONTENTS

FOREWORD

Why does this book exist, and what is The Recipe? Until you know the answers to those two questions, do not buy this book. That means I better let you know right now.

This book exists because I survived depression for 30 years and I found freedom from depression 14 years ago (2009). Now, I wake up every morning excited to be alive. This book is not about beating depression or anxiety, addictions, trauma, or any of that. This book is all about living life with ease, even when life isn't easy.

In this book, I give you a simple recipe for life. It's the one I use every day. The one that transformed my life from merely surviving depression every day to going through the motions from day to day, and then to how I live life now.

How do I live life now? I see every moment of life as a new adventure. Sometimes the adventure is to walk through fields of butterflies, rainbows and unicorns. At other times, the adventure is to carry the One Ring into Mordor. In all cases, I enjoy the adventure!

My motto for life is the way I live life, "Enjoy the Adventure!"

You too can use it to live life with such ease that the root causes of depression, anxiety, PTSD, addictions and much more automatically fade away. As they fade away, your capacity to enjoy the adventure of life grows from moment to moment every day.

Do you need a recipe for life? Well, did anyone ever teach you how to live life with ease?

Do you want to live life with ease?

The Recipe can give that ease to you. Of course, if you like struggle and strain, then The Recipe is not for you.

If, however, you want to enjoy life from moment to moment, if you want to "Enjoy the Adventure!", then The Recipe is for you.

Will it work for you?

I'm a firm believer in "try before you buy." Before you even consider buying this book, open your favorite web browser and go to *RamdasWrites.com/TheRecipe* where you can try some of the techniques. The techniques aren't The Recipe, but I use them to help you experience the effects of The Recipe.

When you try those techniques, notice how you feel before you begin. What is your mental, emotional, and physical state? Then notice how you feel after you finish the technique. If you find you feel more relaxed and at ease, The Recipe will work for you.

More than just reading.

This book is interactive. If you're just going to read it, don't buy it. It won't do you any good.

How is it interactive?

First, after you finish reading this foreword, I'll ask you to imagine that we're having a conversation over a cup of homemade chai. The only time I will refer to this book as a book is here in the foreword. From this point forward, it will simply be our conversation.

Second, throughout our conversation, I'll ask you to experience what we talk about for yourself. I call these activities, *Investigations*, which brings up an important point.

At no time and under no circumstances should you believe me. What does that mean?

I won't lie to you and I won't try to trick you. But if you believe me without question, none of this will work for you. Belief doesn't have the power to change your life.

> "Belief means not wanting to know what is true."
>
> — FRIEDRICH NIETZSCHE

> "To believe in something, and not to live it, is dishonest."
>
> — MAHATMA GANDHI

You must directly experience for yourself how The Recipe works or you'll never be able to use it effectively.

Third, you'll notice throughout our conversation that there's a lot of empty space. This is intentional.

These empty spaces are time for you to write out your thoughts. Describe what you experience through your *Investigations*. You could, and perhaps even should, journal these things. I also encourage you to write them directly into our conversation. Make this conversation a living expression of what you experience.

Our conversation will be exceptionally simple and direct. There's much more for us to talk about, but all of that is too big for this conversation; so, I'll save that for another conversation. Besides, I know you want our conversation to give you something you can use now.

You're on your own, but you're not alone.

The Recipe is incredibly powerful. It can literally change your life, but you have to be the one who uses it. No one can use it for you. That means you're on your own.

Being on your own means you don't have to hope someone on high gives you their blessing. It means you have the power to stand on your own feet. It can also mean that you feel alone and lonely.

Being on your own doesn't require you to be alone or feel lonely. You're on your own, yes. However, you are *not* alone on this journey.

I'm right here with you. I use The Recipe every day.

I've given The Recipe to multitudes of people and they're on this same journey with you as well. There are teenagers and

90-year-olds, homemakers and CEOs, people of all ages and walks of life, all using the techniques in The Recipe.

I'm sure someone warned you about the dangers of peer pressure at some point. Have you ever considered the positive power of peer pressure? One of my teachers put it this way: "Company is stronger than willpower." In other words, peer pressure makes everything easier.

Where can you find this positive peer pressure, this company that is stronger than willpower? You can create your own circle of positive peer pressure by telling others, family and friends, how The Recipe changes your life. You can also find details at *RamdasWrites.com/TheRecipe* for joining a growing online community through social media channels.

Who is this Ramdas?

"Hey look. He's just this guy, ya know?" I'm just some guy who survived 30 years of depression and multiple suicide attempts. In 2014, I discovered I was no longer experiencing depression. In fact, I discovered that I had been depression free for nearly 6 years but hadn't noticed!

Even though I was depression free, I was just living life. It was that thing I did every day and that was about it. Still, it was much easier than all those years of depression. I diligently *investigated* what had caused the transformation I experienced.

My *investigation* led to The Recipe. The Recipe is a starting point, but I've had people testing that starting point for more than 2 years. The transformations they report in their

own lives within just days of using The Recipe are phenom-
enal, but don't believe me and don't believe them. Try it for
yourself.

A CUP OF CHAI

Introduction

Hello and welcome! I'm so glad you're here. Let's talk about The Recipe.

Like all recipes, The Recipe is best when shared with a friend. If you look at the cover, you'll see a comfy couch and a cup of chai or spiced tea on the table. Imagine that you and I are sitting there, about to enjoy a cup of chai together as we talk. In fact, I actually recommend using the chai recipe you'll find at the end of this conversation to make a cup of chai so you can sip while we talk.

If you listened to my introduction over in the foreword, then you already know a little about me. It's also possible you came right here to the kitchen and sat down first; so, let me quickly tell you a little about me.

"Hey look. I'm just this guy, ya know?" which really means, despite all appearances, there's not much difference between you and me. Sure, what we've experienced might be wildly different, but the ones who experienced all of that, you and me, we're not that different.

I've experienced 30 years of depression, which included multiple suicide attempts. I've lived over 14 years now, completely depression free. Every day for the last three years, I've started each day excited to be alive. That part is a bit of a shocker, even to me.

The Recipe allows you to experience relief from the things in your life that disturb your mind now. And, be honest, that's the reason you're here.

Why are you here?

You and I are sitting in this kitchen, sipping chai, and having this conversation because you believe I have some*thing* that can give you relief from whatever is disturbing you.

What makes you think I can help you? I already know you believe I can help you or we wouldn't be sipping chai together. We wouldn't be having this conversation. Right now, however, it's extremely important that you are very clear about why you think I can help you.

You might remember that I said there would be empty space in our conversation and that these empty spaces would provide a time and place for you to write out your thoughts. You have some thoughts about why you believe I can help you. I see an empty space.

Write out your thoughts about why you think I can help you. What you write will help you remember why we're even having this conversation.

I know The Recipe will transform your life.

In the space below or in a journal, write why you believe that as well.

How to use our conversation.

I've already mentioned once that our time together must be interactive. Let's quickly review what that means.

First, this is a conversation. Remember to keep that pictured in your mind, that we're two friends sipping chai together in the kitchen.

Second, your direct participation and experience are vital. When we come to an *Investigation*—you just experienced your first *Investigation*, writing out why you believe The Recipe can help you—do not continue the conversation without investigating first. If you don't investigate, you're stuck believing me and that won't be effective.

Finally, the empty spaces provide a time and place for you to write out your thoughts. This is a form of *Investigation*. Use the empty spaces.

Use. Them.

The Recipe is amazing. Even though it's amazing, it's not the most important ingredient. The most important ingredient is your enthusiasm. To help nurture and increase your enthusiasm, join the growing online community through the social media links at *RamdasWrites.com/TheRecipe*.

You'll find conversations around questions and answers. You might join the conversations where you can report your success stories and listen to the success stories of others. There are also conversations about difficulties using The Recipe. In the near future, there will be opportunities for one-on-one conversations with myself and other mentors.

Still, you have to use The Recipe yourself. There's also lots of encouragement and support available.

Now, we've been talking for a bit. Let's take a short breather and relax for a moment. In fact, our next *Investigation* is exactly that, a short breather.

Before we get to the *Investigation* itself, let me tell you how *Investigations* work. I'll give you all the instructions you need right here in our conversation; however, our conversation requires that you keep your eyes open unless you're listening to my voice right now.

Keeping your eyes open with some of these *Investigations* will make them difficult; so, I've recorded all the instructions for each *Investigation* and they're available on *RamdasWrites. com/TheRecipe*.

Another option is to record yourself reading the instructions. You could also ask someone else to either read the instructions to you or to make a recording of them for you. The least effective use of an *Investigation* is to guide yourself through the instructions live instead of using a recording.

Throughout the instructions for each *Investigation*, you'll notice a line that says [Pause 3—5 breaths] or something similar. If you're making a recording or reading the instructions for someone else, don't read the words within the brackets, [ ].

Investigation #1: A Short Breather

[Visit *RamdasWrites.com/TheRecipe* for a recording of me guiding this *Investigation*]

[If you are using the script to create a private recording, do not read the text between the brackets aloud.]

Sit comfortably with the eyes closed.

If possible, breathe in and out through the nose.

Feel the movement of the chest and belly with each inhale and exhale.

[Pause 3—5 breaths]

On the next inhale, feel the breath flow in through the nostrils.

Follow the sensation of that inhale into the body to where it seems to stop.

Does it stop in the throat, or in the upper chest, or down into the middle chest?

It doesn't matter where the inhale stops.

Follow the sensation of the inhale to where it stops in the body.

Now follow the exhale.

Follow the sensation of the exhale out to about 6 inches in front of the face.

Inhale from that point, 6 inches in front of the face.

Follow the inhale to where it stops in the body.

Exhale, follow the breath out to 6 inches in front of the face.

[Pause 3—5 breaths]

Inhale, follow the breath to where it stops in the body.

Notice, there's a slight pause or hesitation before the exhale naturally begins again.

Follow the breath out to 6 inches in front of the face.

Notice, there's a slight pause or hesitation before the inhale naturally begins.

Focus on these pauses.

Inhale, pause.

Exhale, pause.

[Pause 3—5 breaths]

Notice that as you focus on the pauses, they become just a little longer, a little softer.

[Pause 3—5 breaths]

On the next inhale, listen and feel for the sound, "Hah" but don't actually make the sound.

Just listen and feel for the sound, "Hah" as you inhale.

On the next exhale, listen and feel for the sound, "Sah" but don't actually make the sound.

Just listen and feel for the sound, "Sah" as you exhale.

[Pause 2—3 breaths]

Inhale. Listen and feel for the sound, "Hah", then listen and feel for the sound "mmm" as you feel the pause where the breath stops inside the body.

The inhaling breath now has the silent sound and feel of "Hahmmm."

The exhaling breath has the silent sound and feel of "Sah."

Hahmmm-Sah. Hahmmm-Sah.

Continue with this Hamsa Breath until I ask you to stop.

[Pause 5—15 breaths]

Now let the breath return to its own natural rhythm,

And notice the effect of this short breather.

Notice how relaxed the body is.

Notice how soft the breath is.

Notice how quiet the mind is.

[Pause 3—5 breaths]

On the next inhale, let the inhale draw your attention out to the fingers and toes.

As you feel the fingers and toes, allow them to begin to move.

As the fingers and toes begin to move, allow them to begin moving the hands and feet.

As the hands and feet begin to move, allow them to move the arms and legs until the whole body begins gently moving and stretching.

Once you feel you're totally back in the body, take a moment to review what you noticed.

On rare occasions, some people feel a little agitated or anxious after this *Investigation*. If that happened for you, you did nothing wrong. Anxiety is a coping mechanism that keeps the mind busy and noisy in a belief that the noisy thoughts somehow keep you safe. This *Investigation* quiets the mind, and that sometimes activates anxiety's early warning systems.

If that happened for you, come back to this *Investigation* once a day for the next three days. You'll be surprised by how quickly what you experience in this *Investigation* changes.

Describe your experience in the space below or in your journal.

2

THE BASICS

Problems, We all have them. They are not the most important piece.

I've said it already. You're here to experience relief and you want it now. I understand that. I could just give you The Recipe right now and be done with it, but that wouldn't be very helpful.

As a kid, I wasn't allowed to help in the kitchen and I definitely wasn't allowed to cook anything until I'd had some basic training. You're not a kid, well, you might be, but the same applies. You need some basics before you can use The Recipe.

I'll go through this with enough detail so you can be successful and at the same time, let's not get stuck in the details!

You're here in the kitchen with me sipping chai because you have some problems that feel like they're out of control. Does that sound about right?

Here's some empty space to write your five biggest problems. Don't get stuck in the details, just use a word or two to identify them. If you realize that three or four of your top five problems are relationship issues, lump them all together as relationship issues and write three or four other top problems. If you find that with another category, lump them all together so you have five distinctly different top problems.

What are your problems? Write them out in the space below or in your journal.

NOW THAT WE have that out of the way, let me tell you something interesting about those five problems. Most of your focus is probably on those top-five and how to fix them, right?

As you'll discover in just a minute, those are not the real problem at all. They aren't even problems. They're just distractions. These distractions that are causing you all kinds of problems, sure, but they aren't the real problem. Those are symptoms of the real problem.

Don't worry, The Recipe clears up the symptoms too.

What is a problem?

Before we get to the real problem, let's figure out why those top five feel like problems, even though they aren't.

How do you know that something is a problem? Have you ever thought about that? What makes you think something is a problem?

Here's a little challenge for you. Use just one sentence to describe how you know if something is a problem. Here's some empty space.

In your journal or in the space below, describe how you know if something is a problem. Remember, just one sentence.

NOW LET'S COMPARE NOTES. Have you ever had a problem that you like? Before you answer, I've spent a lot of time working with people in addiction recovery over the years. When I've asked this question, people often say, "Yes, I like my addiction." They also admit that they don't like the collateral damage around it.

So, once again, have you ever had a problem that you like? If you look closely, the answer is always "No." Every problem comes with the feeling of, "*This should not be like this!*" Look at your top five problems/symptoms. They all have that feeling, don't they?

This should not be like this!

It's that feeling of, *This should not be like this!*, that tells you something is a problem. It's that feeling that says you want something to change. Usually, you don't know what needs to change or how to change it. Thankfully, The Recipe is not about changing anything. The Recipe allows life to change itself, but that comes a little later.

Do you want to keep them?

Do you want to keep your top five? Before you say no, ask yourself if you're really willing to live your life without them. What would your life be like if you could never even think about them again?

Take a moment to write out what your life would be like if you could never even think of those top five again and ask yourself if you're willing to live a life like that. A life where you never think about those top five. Write that down too. Are you willing to live such a life?

Using your journal or the space below, write what your life would be like without those top five.

Don't say that!

Let's take this a step further. Do you ever say mean things about yourself? Knowing human nature, that's a silly question. I've never met anyone over the age of 10 who hasn't said something mean about themself.

Whatever it is you typically say, do you want it to be true? Of course you don't want it to be true, but you keep saying it. Every time you say it or think it, you're telling yourself it's true. You're trying to make it true even though you don't want it to be true!

Stop it. You never have to say something that you don't want to be true.

Sometimes we have to talk about things we don't want to be true. Those things are in the past. Put them in the past when you speak about them. I never say, "My depression lasted 30 years." It's not mine, I experienced it but I refuse to carry it with me. I leave it in the past.

What to do?

So what to do? Interrupt the way you think. Change what you say about the past and about yourself.

For example:

I survived 30 years of depression. It's in the past.

In the past, I was very shy. I'm much more outgoing now.

I've lived through a lot of panic attacks. I had one yesterday and I feel much better today.

Take a moment to look at your top five.

Use your journal or the space below to write them into the past, where they belong.

As soon as you catch yourself saying something that you don't want to be true (don't worry, it will happen), stop!

Change whatever you were about to say so it's either positive, say what you want to be true, or make it accurately reflect that whatever you're saying happened in the past. Be doggedly persistent about this. Change what you think or what you say every time you notice it.

Kitchen Magic

Now it's time to teach you some Kitchen Magic.

I already said those top-five problems are really just symptoms. Kitchen Magic reveals that they aren't really problems at all.

First, you need to know about the garbage magic you've been using without even knowing it. Garbage magic has the power to turn heaven into hell. I've already revealed it to you but, you probably didn't recognize it. If you did, great! If you didn't, great! I'll point it out right now.

Garbage magic has only one power, and that power turns heaven to hell. All the power of garbage magic is in these six words:

This should not be like this!

Sometimes we make garbage magic spicy by adding one word: *Dammit!*

So, normal garbage magic is, "*This should not be like this!*" Spicy garbage magic is, "*This should not be like this! Dammit!*" Stop using garbage magic!

Garbage magic turns the littlest inconvenience into a Mount Everest sized problem. Stop using it.

So, what is this Kitchen Magic that turns all problems into situations and circumstances? These four words hold all of Kitchen Magic's power:

This is like this.

Kitchen Magic comes with its own encouraging phrase: *Whether I like it or not.*

Kitchen Magic doesn't remove the circumstance you find yourself in. If the gas tank is empty, saying, "*This is like this.*" doesn't magically fill up the gas tank. You notice the gas tank is empty, and it needs your attention. It's not a problem, it's a situation that needs your attention.

The secret behind Kitchen Magic is that your top five problems are just situations that need your attention. That's all they are.

Don't worry if Kitchen Magic doesn't completely click yet, if you don't quite get it yet. It's not that Kitchen Magic is hard to understand. I'll bet you're seeing how it works already. But that old garbage magic has some pretty strong momentum behind it. Just learning about Kitchen Magic doesn't always immediately remove garbage magic's power and hold over your life but, you can start practicing Kitchen Magic right now.

Here are the simple steps to practicing Kitchen Magic without a license.

1. Notice when a problem has appeared. (You just made a frustrating one appear from memory.)

2. Notice the feeling of garbage magic. It feels like, *"This should not be like this, dammit!"*
3. Use Kitchen Magic to turn the problem into a situation, *"This is like this."*
4. Ask "What does this need from me?"
5. If something is needed, do what is needed.

That's it. That's how you use Kitchen Magic. Kitchen Magic is very strong and powerful. It can turn any problem into a situation. Sometimes, however, the problem you think you see is so strong that Kitchen Magic almost seems powerless. That's why this isn't a conversation about Kitchen Magic.

Nothing is stronger than The Recipe. The Recipe always comes through. It's very tempting to say, "Trust me," but don't. Don't believe me. You'll have time to cook with The Recipe soon enough.

Investigation # 2: Kitchen Magic

Now it's time to practice a little Kitchen Magic as an *Investigation*.

Find something that felt frustrating in the last 24 hours and write it down in the empty space provided.

Really focus on it for a moment, visualize everything that happened. Visualize it so much you can feel the same frustration that you felt when it actually happened. Yes, I'm asking you to intentionally practice a little garbage magic right now.

When you're ready, turn the page and practice some Kitchen Magic without a license.

1. Notice when a problem has appeared. (You just made a frustrating one appear from memory.)
2. Notice the feeling of garbage magic. It feels like, "*This should not be like this, dammit!*"
3. Use Kitchen Magic to turn the problem into a situation, "*This is like this.*"
4. Ask "What does this need from me?"
5. If something is needed, do what is needed.

In the space below or in your journal, write out what was needed from you in this situation.

USING *the space below or your journal, write out the effect of doing what was needed.*

Physics: Energy. What is energy?

If you're going to be cooking, you'll need some heat. What is heat? It's energy, right?

You're constantly surrounded by energy. Einstein said that everything is energy. That's what $E=mc^2$ means. Matter—the table, the chai, you, me, everything—is just energy moving at different speeds.

Without energy, electricity actually, your heart would stop beating and you'd be dead. Your body generates just enough electricity and heat to keep all of its systems functioning.

How energy usually works.

The typical way we use energy makes it move down and out. What does that mean exactly?

When you feel tired, you feel rundown, right? That word, rundown, helps explain the downward movement of energy. You might start with a lot of energy and by the end of the day, you feel rundown. That's natural.

Have you ever felt rundown early in the morning? Why does that happen? That comes from the second movement of energy, out.

Most of the time, you habitually focus your attention outward. You focus on other people. You focus on their needs and their wants and their expectations.

Think back to the short breather *Investigation*. Where did you focus attention most of the time? You didn't focus outward. You focused inward. Yes, you followed the breath out 6 inches in front of the face but you focused there for only a moment and then you moved your attention back inside.

How did you feel at the end of that *Investigation*? Did you feel rundown or did you feel relaxed, rested or maybe even a little energized? For a moment, you changed the movement of energy in you from down and out to inward and maybe even upward.

Energy follows attention.

Have you ever felt angry? Of course you have, so have I.

Have you ever noticed what happens when you focus on feeling angry? The anger gets bigger, doesn't it? If you focus on it hard enough, you can work yourself right up into a fit.

What you focus on gets bigger. Energy follows your attention. In the short breather *Investigation*, you focused attention mainly inward. Your internal energy, in the form of attention, wasn't streaming out into the world. It was recycling back into your own body.

Whatever you focus on gets bigger. This is why I don't want you to say anything mean or untrue about yourself. I don't even want you to say anything about others that is mean or untrue, but let's start with just you.

If you need to say something about the past, make sure you put it in the past. Don't feed it in the present. Don't bring it back to life now. Leave it in the past.

Let's use what you've just recognized about energy to your advantage.

Think back to what you felt at the end of the short breather Investigation. Use one or two words to name what you felt. If you felt relaxed, then your word is relaxed. If you felt peaceful, then your word is peaceful. If you felt agitated or anxious, that happens once in a while. Remember to repeat the *Investigation* once a day over the next three days and then find your word.

Every time you find yourself about to say something mean or untrue, interrupt it. Replace what you were about to say with the word you just identified. I encourage you to say, "I am relaxed," or whatever your specific word is out loud each time you start to say something mean or untrue about yourself or anyone else.

If you don't feel comfortable saying it out loud, just say it in your head and then continue on with what you need to say.

Can you guess what I'm about to suggest? If you said write about using your new phrase to replace mean or untrue things, you were right!

What is your new phrase? What would life be like if you were already living your life that way? Use the space provided or your journal to explore these questions.

MORE SPACE

How to use Time

Every good chef knows how to use a kitchen timer. Speaking of timer, how long have we been sitting here? What time is it?

Did you check a clock to see what time it is? Have you ever checked a clock to see what time it is? Of course you have.

Regardless of the time the clock shows, have you ever experienced a time that wasn't Now? You might be tempted to say the past. But when the past was happening, wasn't it Now?

We talk about the past, present and future all the time. "All the time" (chuckle). Seriously though, past, present and future, that's time, right? But have you ever experienced a time that wasn't Now?

No, of course not. Now is the only time that exists. But, don't believe me! Let's check it out together and see if that's actually true.

Living in the Past

Have you ever heard the phrase, "Living in the past?" Sure. It's a common phrase. What does it mean? It could mean that a person is old-fashioned or is trying to relive their youth. Maybe they're having a flashback to a traumatic event.

But, are any of them actually reliving the past or is the past affecting the present?

That's what it really means. The past, which is only a memory, is affecting the present.

What is a memory, by the way? It's just a thought about a thing or event that happened in the past and isn't present now. It has no reality other than the thought in your mind. Every time you replay that memory, that thought about the past, you take it out of the graveyard of the past and bring it back to life.

It's zombies!

Seriously though, it's very possible for the past to affect the present, but when is it actually happening? It's happening Now. Remember that it's always happening Now. That will be very important soon.

Castles in the Sky

"Soon" that one word brings us to the future. What is it really? Are we in the future now? Or are we still in Now? It's still Now. It can only be Now.

Have you ever used dreams of the future to escape from what's happening Now? Daydreams, we all have them. Nothing wrong with daydreams.

Notice that daydreams move energy down and out. They use up the energy, maybe only to a small degree, that we need to live now.

No matter how far into the future you dream, when's the only time you experience that dream? It's Now. It's always Now. Literally, it's always Now!

Now is eternal. Eternity is a time that has no beginning or end. Does Now have a beginning? When I ask this question, many people say, "Yes." If Now has a beginning, that means at some point it has to stop so it can begin again.

Does Now ever end? No one ever answers, "Yes," to that question. Now never ends. If Now never ends, then that also means Now never begins. It is always Now. That is eternity.

You're living in eternity. Crazy, right?

Four Arrows

You can only live now, and you have always lived in now. You will only ever live now.

Now is all there is, but how familiar are you with Now? You need to have a very clear understanding of Now for The Recipe to work.

The best way to understand Now is using the four arrows of time.

Imagine that you're shooting arrows at a target. You have a quiver full of arrows to shoot. The first arrow is still in the quiver. You have another one arrow notched and ready to shoot. A third arrow flies through the air toward the target and a fourth arrow is already stuck in the target. These are the four arrows of time.

The first arrow we'll look at is the one in the target. That arrow represents the past. It's already happened and you can't change where it will hit the target. That's easy to understand. The past is unchangeable. The arrow already hit the target.

Now, let's look at the quiver full of arrows. These arrows have unlimited possibility. You can shoot them at the target or you can turn around and shoot them in another direction. You can even leave them in the quiver and use them on an entirely different day. These arrows represent the future. They are full of unlimited possibilities.

Past and future, target and quiver, easy to understand. So far, so good.

Let's look at the arrow flying through the air. That arrow is Now. It's happening. Can you change where that arrow will hit the target? No, of course not and despite what all the cartoons say about shooting another arrow really fast, it will never be fast enough to hit the arrow flying through the air and change its course. It's clear that you can't change the arrow flying through the air, right?

The last arrow is the one you have notched and ready to shoot. It's also full of *unlimited* possibility. We could say that it's not quite full of unlimited possibility, because you've already notched it. You can also shoot it in whatever direction you want or just hold it for a while.

The only possibility that's unavailable is leaving it in the quiver. You already took it out of the quiver. You can put it back in the quiver, but you can't change the past; so you can't undo taking it out of the quiver. That one potential no longer exists, but other than that one potential, you have unlimited freedom, unlimited potential, in that arrow and what you do with it.

These are the four arrows of time. The *past* is in the target. The *future* is in the quiver. *Now* is flying through the air. And *what's next* is the notched arrow.

Past and future are easy to understand. There's not really much mystery there. There's infinite potential in the future, but nothing too mysterious. Those two arrows in the middle; however, we need to look at them a little more closely. And when we do, it will change the way you under-stand Now forever and that's a good thing.

Here's my hand drawn version of the four arrows hours of time.

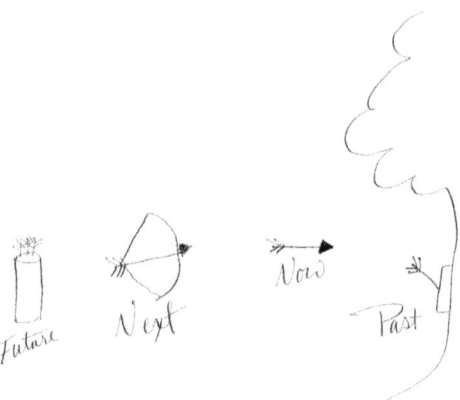

Use a piece of paper, your journal or the space below to draw your own version of the four arrows of time!

Unchangeable Now

What's so special about those two arrows, *Now* and *next*, that will change the way you see Now forever?

Let's examine that arrow called *Now*. It's flying through the air. There's nothing you can do to change its course. You are powerless to alter the trajectory of that arrow.

A gust of wind might come up and change its course. A bird might fly into it and that would change its course. A meteor might fall from the sky and crash into the arrow. That would definitely change its course! But *you* can do nothing to change its course.

This seems to be saying that you can't change Now. Is that true?

Can you change Now?

Think about that for a moment before continuing our conversation. Really work it out in your own mind. Can you change Now?

Most people, when I ask this question, say, "Yes. Of course I can change Now." This next example usually clears up that misunderstanding.

If I decide to turn the light on now, is the light on Now or do I have to walk to the wall and flip the light switch? Obviously, I have to walk to the wall to turn the light switch.

No matter how fast I turn the light switch on, it happens after I make the decision. It happens a moment after Now and then it becomes part of Now.

All action happens Now but any action can only change what's next. The result always appears after. It doesn't change Now. It changes a moment from Now.

I can shoot that next arrow in any way I want. It never changes the arrow flying through the air Now. It only determines how the next arrow will fly through the air Now.

The only way that I can change Now, that arrow flying through the air, is to change what happened a moment ago. I have to change the past so that Now shows up differently than it is Now. That. Is. Impossible.

Now is unchangeable.

Do not continue our conversation until those previous three words are absolutely clear. Repeat the four arrows and this part of our conversation a few times if you need to and then we'll move on.

Now is unchangeable.

Are you clear that Now is unchangeable? Don't worry, just because Now is unchangeable doesn't mean you're stuck. It actually means you're free but I don't want to get ahead of things. Just focus on this new understanding that Now is unchangeable.

In your journal on using this space, write down your thoughts about this new understanding of Now.

MORE SPACE

Now is Perfect

We're not done with that flying arrow yet. Now that you know that now is unchangeable, I can tell you something that might seem shocking about that flying arrow.

This part often feels a little difficult for people when they first encounter it. I promise, once you fully understand this next piece, it will make those top five just a little lighter.

Now is always perfect.

Did your mind just come up with reasons why that's not true? I'll bet it even went to your number one item on the top five as an example of Now not being perfect. That's OK. That's because we're using the word "perfect" just a little differently from each other.

If I say the word "Rose" what comes to mind? A flower? What color flower? Was it red or pink or yellow? Maybe it was orange? Perhaps you noticed I emphasized "Rose". Maybe that made you think of a person, but what person?

In my mind, I am thinking of a wonderful redheaded artist friend of mine. Her last name is Rose. If we aren't using a word in the same way, we won't be able to understand each other. So, what do I mean when I say that Now is always perfect?

For most people, perfect really means, "It is the way I think it should be." In this sense, my version of perfect weather includes a thunderstorm and the first snowfall. Your version of perfect weather might be a sunny day.

Again, what do I mean when I say now is always perfect? I mean that now is always perfect in the same way that 2+2 = 4 is always perfect. The number 4 is the perfect result of adding 2 and 2.

Now is always the perfect result of what just happened. Now is always perfect whether I like the way it shows up or not.

Let's get extreme with this. Think of the most challenging day you have ever experienced, the worst day of your life. That day was perfect. It was the perfect result of every moment before it. That doesn't mean it was an experience you liked.

I guarantee it was an experience you didn't like because you still think of it as the worst day of your life. You call it the worst day of your life because something horrible happened. The feeling of, "*This should not be like this, dammit!*" was extreme! It probably still feels extreme or you wouldn't still think of it as the worst day of your life. All of that is true. It's also true that the day was the perfect result of everything that came before it.

On that day, you showed up the only way you could. On that day, everyone else showed up the only way they could. That's the definition of perfect. That is 2+2 = 4. You don't have to like what happened. I don't have to like what happened.

All we have to remember is that Now is happening the only way it can. It is always the perfect result of what came before it. That doesn't mean that it's always a happy Now. And this is not permission for you or for me or for anyone else to be a jackass. It simply recognizes that we are all showing up the only way we can now.

Now is unchangeable.

Now is always perfect.

The past always controls people who don't know this. But don't believe me! Verify it for yourself. Has the past ever seemed to control you? Has a bad day yesterday ever made today bad as well?

Of course it has! The past will always control those who don't know that Now is perfect.

But Now you know how much control the past has on the present. You also know that Now is perfect. That means you already have a little more freedom to use the other arrows with their infinite potential.

Why does this give you more freedom to use that infinite potential? Because you know that trying to change the past or to even change what's happening NOW is a waste of time and energy. They can't be changed. Instead of trying to change them, you can put all of your energy toward what needs to happen next.

This is another great time to write out what you're experiencing.

What's next?

It's not quite time for The Recipe yet. You're still missing one ingredient. Still, this new understanding of now can transform your Kitchen Magic. Let's quickly review how to practice Kitchen Magic without a license.

1. Notice when a problem has appeared.
2. Notice the feeling of garbage magic. It feels like, *"This should not be like this, dammit!"*

3. Use Kitchen Magic to turn the problem into a situation, "*This is like this.*"
4. Ask "What does this need from me?"
5. If something is needed, do what is needed.

How does knowing that now is unchangeable super charge your Kitchen Magic? You now know that now is unchangeable and is always perfect (whether we like it or not).

If now is unchangeable and perfect, doesn't that actually make step number 2 a bit sillier? I actually like to shake my fist at the sky and say a bit of garbage magic out loud, "*This should not be like this, dammit!*", because it always makes me laugh when I do.

What I'm really saying is, "*I don't like this, dammit!*" I feel like a whiny little kid when I do, and it just makes me laugh. Then when I use step number 3, it's so much more powerful because of the laugh. It's actually a relief to say, "*This is like this.*"

Special investigation # 3: Supercharged Kitchen Magic

For this *Special Investigation*, our conversation must come to a temporary stop.

For the next 24 hours, you need to practice supercharged Kitchen Magic, and this requires you to be especially attentive. It requires your dogged persistence.

Every time you notice that you seem to be experiencing a problem, you must practice your Kitchen Magic. Every time. If you don't notice right away, as soon as you notice, it's Kitchen Magic time!

Here're the steps again:

1. Notice when a problem appears.
2. Notice the feeling of garbage magic. It feels like,
3. *"This should not be like this, dammit!"*
4. Shake a fist for a little supercharging.
5. Use Kitchen Magic to turn the problem into a situation,
6. *"This is like this."*
7. Give the situation the attention it needs if appropriate.

Every time you use Kitchen Magic over the next 24 hours, make a note. Put your notes here in our conversation. You must verify if this works or if I'm just trying to pull the wool over your eyes.

I suggest setting a timer on your phone as well, like every 47 minutes. Whenever the timer goes off, apply Kitchen Magic to whatever's happening. Also, remember to apply Kitchen Magic to every problem that seems to appear.

I'll see you tomorrow for some more conversation and chai.

Use your journal or this space to write out what happened during your Investigation. What worked well and what needs refining?

EVEN MORE SPACE

3

WHO ARE YOU?

Do you know who you are?

Welcome back! How did the *Special Investigation* go? Don't worry if you weren't 100% successful. This was your first time using Kitchen Magic. Each time you use it, it'll be easier and more powerful. Of course, soon, we'll turn that Kitchen Magic into The Recipe.

Now for the most important question and the most important answers. By the way, how's your chai? I made a fresh cup for myself just before you walked in.

Back to the most important question. Do you know who you are?

Who are you?

Here are some common answers to this seemingly simple question that is really the most important one you can ever ask. Many people give their name as their answer. Other people put down their jobs or their education or their relationships or some other descriptions. What will your answer or answers be?

In your journal or this space, write your answer or answers to this most important question: Who are you?

Do you change?

Does who you are seem to change from moment to moment or from circumstance to circumstance? Do you seem to be one person with this group of friends and another person with those coworkers? And someone entirely different depending on which family members are present?

Who are you?

Do you ever feel like a chameleon changing who you are from moment to moment to moment?

Even if you seem to change who you are from moment to moment, from circumstance to circumstance, do you actually change? Are you a different person in different circumstances or is it always you just playing different characters on the stage of life?

Are you sure?

Now that we've talked a bit about this most important question, "Who are you?", are you sure that you know who you are?

You already know that our conversation is full of surprises. Just think about what happened to your understanding of Now while we were talking yesterday.

Today we're going to look at who you are just as closely as we looked at Now when we talked yesterday.

If you feel ready, have a sip of chai and let's get started.

Who are you?

I'm about to get a little pokey. What does that mean? It means I'm going to poke at the answers you wrote when I asked you, "Who are you?"

Did you write more than one answer? If you did, that means you don't know who you are. Because there's only one of you, right? If there's only one of you, there can't be multiple answers to the question, "Who are you?"

If you answered with your name, who gave you that name? Did you not exist before they gave you that name?

Or, were you clever and wrote something like Love or a Being of Light or a child of God? Is that what you feel when you're introduced to someone new? Do people introduce you and say, "This is Kim, our resident Being of Light." Do you introduce yourself that way? Do you think of yourself that way if someone doesn't ask a question like, "Who are you?" If the answer isn't yes, you have a concept of who you are and, yet, you don't know who you are, you don't feel it.

Some of you have had this conversation with me before and so you have that concept of who you are, but do you feel it at all times?

If you don't feel it at all times, you still don't know who you are. You have the right idea, but it hasn't become the way you live life yet. You don't yet *know* it.

Have a sip of chai and let's investigate who you are.

Investigation #4: Slow Motion Energy

[Visit *RamdasWrites.com/TheRecipe* for a recording of me guiding this Investigation.]

[If you are using the script to create a private recording, do not read the text between the brackets.]

This *Investigation* requires you to be supremely comfortable. Sit in a supremely comfortable position and also make sure that you are sitting attentively. I suggest sitting on a kitchen chair with a small pillow between your low back and the back of the chair. You might also place a cushion under your feet. This will help you sit up and allow you to feel supremely comfortable as you sit.

Rest the hands on the knees or thighs with the palms facing up. In a moment, I'll ask you to use your imagination to visualize breathing in and out through different parts of the body; so, let the eyes close and feel the breath gently flowing in and out through the nose.

Long, slow inhales.

Slow, soft exhales.

[Pause 3 breaths]

On the inhale, follow the breath in to where it feels like the inhale stops inside the body.

Notice the familiar pause.

On the exhale, follow the breath out to about 6 inches in front of the face.

Again, notice the familiar pause.

[Pause 3 to 5 breaths]

Now, imagine there's a small opening in the belly just above the navel.

Inhale, feel the belly expand and the chest rise.

Exhale. Visualize and feel the breath flow down and out through the opening in the belly.

Inhale through the nose and exhale down and out through the belly.

Inhale nose, exhale belly.

[Pause 3 breaths]

As you exhale through the belly, imagine that you can now also inhale through the belly.

Inhale belly. Exhale belly.

Imagine the sensations you would feel around the opening at the belly as you breathe in and out through the belly.

Imagine those sensations so clearly you can feel them as you breathe in and out through the belly.

If you're not sure that you're feeling any sensations around the opening at the belly, simply take one or two fingers and touch where you've imagined the opening at the belly.

Make a little circular motion with the fingers.

Feel the sensations at the belly and then let the hand return to the knee or thigh.

Imagine and feel breath flowing in and out through the sensations at the belly.

[Pause 3 breaths]

As you exhale through the belly, bring attention to the center of the chest.

Imagine a small opening at the center of the chest, about the level of the heart.

Inhale through the belly and as you exhale, feel the breath and sensation rise up along the spine to the heart center and exit through the small opening in the chest.

Inhale through the belly.

Exhale through the chest.

Immediately notice the sensations that show up around the opening at the center of the chest, as you breathe in through the belly and out through the center of the chest.

Inhale belly. Exhale chest.

[Pause 3–5 breaths]

On the next exhale through the chest, allow the opening at the belly to close.

Inhale through the chest and exhale through the chest.

The breathing pattern now is: inhale chest and exhale chest.

Notice how the sensations subtly change as you inhale through the chest and exhale through the chest.

[Pause 3–5 breaths]

As you exhale through the chest, shift attention to the palms and imagine an opening, one in the center of each palm.

Inhale through the chest and as you exhale, feel the breath rise up to the shoulders, stream down the arms and exit the openings, one in the palm of each hand.

The breathing pattern now is: inhale chest, exhale palms.

Notice the sensations beginning to arise around the centers of the palms as you inhale through the chest and exhale through the palms.

[Pause 3–5 breaths]

As you exhale through the palms, allow the opening at the chest to close.

Inhale through the palms and exhale through the palms.

The breathing pattern now is: inhale palms and exhale palms.

Feel the sensations arising around the centers of the palms as you gently breathe in and out through the centers of the palms.

[Pause 3–5 breaths]

On the next inhale, allow the hands and forearms to begin slowly drifting up into the air.

As the hands and forearms come off the knees or thighs, allow them to rotate so the palms are facing one another.

Allow the hands to slowly move toward each other without allowing them to touch.

The moment you begin to feel sensation, perhaps a magnetic pressure, between the hands, let them stop.

When the hands stop, let them move away from each other until you feel a subtle pressure or sensation on the back of the hands and let them stop.

Allow the hands to slowly, gently move back and forth, allowing them to explore the sensations between the hands and on the backs of the hands.

[Pause 2 breaths]

If you're not sure whether you are feeling sensation between the hands or on the backs of the hands, let the movement stop.

Allow the hands to move very slowly back and forth, just an eighth of an inch, just a millimeter or two.

Move so slowly you can feel the subtle sensation on the palms and on the backs of the hands.

As soon as you feel that sensation, allow the movement to become larger, but still moving slowly.

[Pause 3–5 breaths]

Now shift attention and notice how quiet, how empty the mind is.

Shift attention back to the sensation in the hands as they move back and forth.

On the next exhale, allow the hands to drift slowly back down to knees or thighs.

Again, shift attention to the mind and notice how quiet, how empty it is.

As you exhale, allow the openings in the palms to close.

Inhale through the nose, exhale through the nose and open the eyes.

Open your eyes.

Notice how relaxed the body is.

Notice how soft breath is.

Notice how silent the mind is.

Rest in this silence and stillness for a few moments before continuing this *Investigation*.

Investigation #4 continued: The 1st Key

[The *Investigation* continues here.]

[Visit *RamdasWrites.com/TheRecipe* for a recording of me guiding this Investigation.]

Could you feel the sensations between your hands? Did your eyes pop right open at the end, or did it take some effort? Pretty amazing, wasn't it? That's not even the good part yet.

Did you notice how quiet, empty even, your mind was? The first time I asked you to notice how empty your mind was, did you find any thoughts in there like "Where're my car keys?" or "Did I leave the stove on?"

For most people, the immediate answer is, "No. There were no thoughts in there." A few people say, "Yes. I had a thought."

If you found a thought, was the thought crazy and loud and right in your face? "Hey, look at me, I'm a thought!" Or was it more like this: I asked you to shift attention and there was a pause and then you noticed a thought? Was it more like one or two?

Of course, it was like the second.

You heard my direction to notice how empty the mind was. You shifted attention and there was a brief pause before you noticed a thought.

If your mind was empty, that just means the pause was big and easily recognizable. If you noticed a thought, that just means the pause was smaller. Let's focus on that pause, big or small, between my directions and any thought that might have appeared.

In that pause, the mind was empty. Were there any thoughts in that empty mind? No, of course not. It was empty, and that's why there was a pause.

Were there any things in that empty pause? Were there any pink unicorns or elephants in there? Of course not, it was empty! If there were things, they would have to be thoughts and there were no thoughts. If there were things, it wouldn't be empty.

Don't just believe me, verify this through your own experience that there was nothing in that pause. If you're not clear on that, go back and experience the guided part of the *Investigation* again.

So, there were no thoughts or things in that gap, that pause. As you looked into that empty gap, did you know your age or gender? No, those would be thoughts and there were no thoughts.

As you looked into that gap, were you even aware of your body? Look back, reflect on your memory. Were you even aware of your body? If you were thinking, "Yeah, I could feel my sore back. That was what I noticed after I looked into the mind." Recognize that was a thought that came after the empty gap. In the empty gap, you weren't aware of any part of the body, let alone if it was sore. That thought came later maybe, but in the gap even that was absent.

It's also possible that the thought, sore back or other body part, was constant. That means you weren't supremely comfortable. If that is the case, get supremely comfortable and then repeat the investigation. In my experience, even people with chronic pain find the pain vanishes in the gap. That could easily be your experience as well.

Let's get back to that empty gap.

Close your eyes for a moment and drop into that empty, quiet gap where there are no thoughts. Now, allow your attention to move forward. Do you run into your forehead? Or can attention keep moving forward, forward, forward, through the wall and over the yard, all the way out to the horizon and even beyond? Feel it.

Now bring attention back to the center and send it off to the right. Does it run into your ear or does it seem to keep going, going, going, going, going? Come back to the center and go off to the left. Do you ever find your left ear? Even if you do, is it a wall that stops attention from continuing to move on and on and on?

Could you find any edges, any limitations or boundaries in that gap? Or did it seem vast and spacious? I know from my experience that it feels vast and spacious in there, doesn't it?

Open your eyes again and let's recap what we've found so far.

Between my directions and any thought that arose, there was an empty gap. In that empty gap, there were no thoughts, no things, no age, no gender, no body, and it had no edges.

When you look into that gap, is your name in there? Is there any answer you gave to the question, "Who are you?" in there? No. The gap is empty. Right?

No thoughts. No things. No age. No gender. No body. No edges. And no you!

One last question, was everything you think of as your history or your hopes and dreams or your fears and doubts, were any of those in the empty gap?

No. The gap was empty.

OK, that's a little weird, right? Did you cease to exist? Of course not, we're still having this conversation.

WHO ARE YOU?!

In that gap, you didn't cease to exist, but nothing you think of as "YOU" was present in that empty gap. If nothing you think of as you was present in the gap, what was looking into that empty gap?

What was looking into the gap? What is that?

That's the real you, not all the stuff you wrote as an answer to, "Who are you?" But what is that real you? It's awareness. It's consciousness. It's "I".

Usually when you answer the question, "Who are you?" You say something like, "I am _____." You focus on the word that comes after "am", which is usually a what, something you do, and it doesn't tell anyone anything about "I".

Who are you really? *I.* That's who you are. And this *I* is vast and unlimited. You are that *I.*

I know this is probably really new. You just found out that who you are is not who you think you are. That doesn't mean that all the things you've thought or experienced are imaginary. It just means they aren't you.

Let's investigate this just a little more and then we'll dive into The Recipe itself.

But first, make a few notes about what you just experienced either in your journal or in this space.

Investigation #5: If you can see it.....

[Visit *RamdasWrites.com/TheRecipe* for a recording of me guiding this Investigation.]

[If you are using the script to create a private recording, do not read the text between the brackets.]

I would like to suggest that if you can see it, you can't be it. This goes right along with the experience you just had; so that may already make sense. Still, it's useful to really give you the feel of what you just experienced.

If you can see it, you can't be it. But don't believe me, let's investigate it.

Look around you and find a houseplant, or any other plant. Look at the plant. Notice its leaves, its branches or stems and any flowers that it might have.

Are you the house plant? If you think you are the house plant; we need to have an entirely different conversation. You are not the house plant. So far, so good. If you can see it, you can't be it.

Now, look at your right hand. Are you your right hand?

You might be tempted to say yes. But, if I cut your right hand off, do you cease to exist? No. You are not your hand. If you can see, you can't be it.

What about your body? You just had an experience where you couldn't find your body and you didn't cease to exist. Are you your body? From your own experience a moment ago, you know you are not your body, but you might notice some resistance to that right now.

If I start removing body parts, how much of the body needs to be removed before you cease to exist? Not how much needs to be removed before the body dies, but how much causes you to cease to be you?

You are not your body. If you can see it, you can't be it.

What about your thoughts? Those were the first thing we noticed were absent in the previous *Investigation*. Are you your thoughts? No. Can you see your thoughts? Think of a pink unicorn or a rose of any color. Can you see it? Of course you can.

You don't see it with your eyes, but you don't really see anything with your eyes. The eyes just send information to the brain. The brain creates a picture out of the information the eyes send it. You see your thoughts with the same mind that creates images from the data the eyes take in.

You can see your thoughts.

You are not your thoughts. Say it with me,

"If you can see it, you can't . . . ."

(Did you say "be it" to yourself just now?)

What about memories? Are you your memories? This is the one where most say, "Yes."

Your previous experience with, "Who are you?" points to the answer being no, that you are not your memories, but what do you feel right now? Are you your memories? If you have the feeling of yes, it's OK. We'll look at memories more closely and even if you have the feeling of no, it will help strengthen that recognition.

What is a memory? What are memories made out of? Have you ever thought about that?

A memory is not an event, nor is it an experience. It's a thought about something that happened in the past. A memory is a thought about the past that is not happening now.

You've already recognized that you are not your thoughts and now you recognize memories are just a type of thought.

You can also see your memories. Bring up your favorite memory and you can see it in detail. You can even make it so vivid that you can smell the smells and taste the tastes associated with it, if you want.

Are you your memories? No, you can't be. They're just thoughts. They don't have any reality outside of your mind. If you can see it, you can't be it.

This one's a little easier. Are you your imagination? What is imagination? It's a thought about the future or about some *thing* that has no reality—pink unicorns dancing with hippos in tutus.

You are not your imagination. If you can see it, you can't be it.

Here's the last one, and it's a biggie: **YOUR HISTORY**

Can you see your history? Of course you can. It's made out of memories. You can see it. You can't be it. Soak in that for a moment.

Take a moment to write what that feels like, what it feels like to know that you are not your history. After you write what you feel, we'll unpack it all.

WRITE *in this space or your journal what you feel now that you know you are not your history?*

Unpacking It All

Phew! That's a lot to take in, isn't it? Sometimes people feel immense relief knowing they're not their history. That usually means they've been carrying a heavy load for a long time.

Others feel a sense of sadness or loss. They have happy memories and there's often a little fear that there aren't any new happy times coming in the future or that any future happy times just won't be as good.

The last group feels a little of both, it's bittersweet. There's relief that they aren't all of that crazy history and there's sadness that they aren't all of that happy history.

Which group do you seem to fall into? And just notice if the way I've described it is accurate for what you feel, too.

If you feel relief, there's not much for us to unpack. Just feel that relief.

If you feel bitter sweet or sadness, notice that you're trying to hold on to the past, those past happy memories. The only place those memories exist, the only reality they have, is in your head, in your thoughts. They aren't real. You can't taste them, touch them, smell them or feel them. You can imagine that you do, but you don't, really.

Remember the four arrows? Remember the arrows in the quiver and the one you're about to shoot? Do you remember I said they were full of infinite possibilities?

Yes? Good.

If those arrows are full of infinite possibilities, doesn't that have to include happiness? It does, doesn't it?

When you live life believing that you are your history, that you are all the thoughts, things, age, gender, body, limitations and history, then, those arrows are not full of infinite possibility. They're only filled with the possibilities contained in the things you think you are.

You've discovered that you are none of those things. You are "*I*"! And "*I*" is not limited by any of those things. "*I*" swims in infinite possibilities. You are that *I*. You are full of infinite possibilities.

Feel that. Say it out loud. "I am full of infinite possibilities."

Say it even louder. "I AM FULL OF INFINITE POSSIBILITIES!"

Here's an empty space full of infinite possibilities. Use it or your journal. Write what that feels like. Do it right now.

MORE SPACE

4

THE RECIPE!

Preparation: Problems make you feel powerless.

Problems can easily make you feel powerless. Thankfully, Kitchen Magic turns all problems into ordinary situations. It's vital that you keep practicing your Kitchen Magic.

Your history can also make you feel trapped and powerless. Thankfully, you've just discovered that you're not your history. It's not even your history! You don't own it. It's just a story that you lived through.

Sometimes that story is a magical fairy tale. At other times, it might've been a horror story. It's all just a story. History even has that word, "story," built into the word "history". So, when you think about history, throw a little kitchen style magic at it and say, "Hi story!" Remind yourself it's just a story.

You are POWERFUL

The reality is, you are powerful. What proof do I have of that? Even more important, what proof do you have of that? Shall I tell you what the most powerful proof of your power is?

You are alive.

If you weren't powerful, the horrible parts of the story you lived through would have killed you. They didn't. In fact, they couldn't.

Now you're even more powerful because you're recognizing the infinite possibilities of "*I*" that exist *Now*.

The Recipe takes the power of Kitchen Magic and combines it with the infinite possibilities of *I-Now*.

Deceptively simple

The Recipe is deceptively simple. When I show it to you in just a moment, it might tempt you to think that it won't work. Something so simple can't be as powerful as I claim it is.

You have to try it out first.

So, let's go through each piece and then we'll put it all together.

You might want to go make some more chai. I think I'm actually going to go make a cup of Earl Grey and then we'll get started.

The Recipe has two parts: The Setup and The Steps.

TADA! This is like this.

The Setup part of the recipe is the Kitchen Magic you've already learned:

This is like this.

It works just like it's been working for you so far. So, it's so important for you to practice your Kitchen Magic every day.

Kitchen Magic stops you from wasting precious energy on trying to change the past. Trying to change the past is a waste of time and energy, PERIOD. Don't do it. Use Kitchen Magic instead.

The Recipe always starts with Kitchen Magic. As soon as you recognize that some garbage magic is happening, "*This should not be like this, dammit!*", immediately apply Kitchen Magic!

This is like this.

Who

As I said, Kitchen Magic is not the first step. It's The Setup. It clears the counter and gives you room to work.

The first step is to ask this question:

Who is experiencing this?

You and I are having this conversation right now. Who is experiencing this? You might be tempted to say, "We are", because we're both experiencing this conversation. But, are you experiencing this conversation the same way I am? Absolutely not. That's impossible.

Who is the only one experiencing this? The answer is always "*I.*" Not the answers you wrote to that question, "Who are you?" The answer is always the real "*I*" that you are.

***Who is experiencing this? I* or *I Am*.** Pick which one works best for you and that is the only answer to this question, forever. For-E-Ver.

When you try to answer, "You're experiencing this.", it's because you're watching someone else experience something and you're looking at the wrong part of who is experiencing what.

Imagine my child tells me they're depressed. If I ask, "Who is experiencing this?" and then answer they are, I'm focusing on something or someone over which I have no influence. I have no influence over what they experience. I can't shoot their arrows. It's not that shooting someone else's arrows is against the rules, it's simply impossible.

If my child tells me they're depressed, the only experience I have influence over is receiving that information from my child. Always focus on what you directly experience.

"Dad, I feel depressed."

This is like this. (My child is telling me something important.)

I. ***Who is experiencing this? I*** (experience my child telling me something important.)

When

The second step is to ask this question:

When am I experiencing this?

Again, there's only one answer to this question and I'm sure you've already guessed the answer. It's *Now*.

Kitchen Magic keeps you from wasting time and energy trying to change the past. Asking this question keeps you anchored in *Now*.

Imagine for a moment that you're experiencing some sort of flashback. The common way of thinking about that is you're reliving the past, but are you? No, you're experiencing the past affecting the present and when is that happening? *Now*.

The mind wants to say, "Well, this made me feel horrible when I was six years old." So what? You can't do anything about what happened when you were six years old. What effect is it having *Now*? What are you experiencing *Now*? That's the only thing that matters.

Does six-year-old you exist *Now*? Some people will go on and on about the inner child and so forth, but show me six-year-old you. The only place the six-year-old-you exists is in your thoughts and we've already examined thoughts and they aren't real. They don't have a reality.

What you are experiencing *Now* has a reality. You can feel it. Yes, you might be feeling the leftovers from what happened when you were six, but you are feeling those leftovers *Now*. Focus on what you experience *Now* because nothing else matters. The past doesn't matter because you can't do anything with it. *Now* matters because you can do everything with it.

I know that everything I just said might seem like I'm telling you to ignore the past and, to be honest, I am, but I am not asking you to ignore the effect of the past. No. I am asking you to focus on the only place you can do anything with those effects, *Now*.

Later, we'll talk about how this works with trauma.

"Dad, I feel depressed."

This is like this. (My child is telling me something important.)

1. ***Who is experiencing this? I*** (experience my child telling me something important.)

2. ***When am I experiencing this?*** Now (my child is telling me something important *Now*.)

What

It's time for step #3. Are you ready?

The third step is to ask this question:

What does Now need from me?

There are two very special answers to this question. It's an either or question.

The first answer is always, "***Nothing***." That's also the answer people usually try to avoid. Some people say, "No, I would rather do nothing. That's the answer I always give myself." The reality is they're using the answer, "***Nothing***," to avoid asking, "What does Now need from me?" They default to

"*Nothing*" so they can pretend nothing needs their attention.

If the answer isn't, "*Nothing*," then it has to be . . . . ?

Can you guess what it is?

Did you guess, "*Something*"? The answer is always *Nothing* or *Something*. Always check to see if *Nothing* is the correct answer first.

Obvious and Immediate

So, it seems like this third question has too much wiggle room in it. How do you know if the answer is really *Nothing*? If the answer is *Something*, how do you know what that *Something* is?

The answer is *Nothing* if there is literally nothing you can do about it right *Now*. There are dishes behind me that need to be washed, but I'm also having this conversation with you. If I look at the dishes, it's obvious that they're dirty and I need to wash them. However, *Now* requires that I continue the conversation with you.

That means there's *Nothing* I can do about the dishes that need to be washed *Now*. Our conversation isn't an excuse to avoid the dishes. When we finish this conversation, I can turn to the dishes and that points out some very important qualities.

The need is obvious, but it isn't immediate.

If something is the correct answer, it will always have two qualities. It will always be both *Obvious* and *Immediate*. The dishes are *Obvious* but they aren't *Immediate*.

When you ask, *"What does Now need from me?"*, look around you and see if there is an *Obvious* and *Immediate Something* for you to do. If there is nothing *Obvious* and *Immediate*, then *Nothing* is the correct answer.

If I walk into a room and see a basket full of dirty laundry and ask, *"What does Now need from me?"*, it would seem *Obvious* and *Immediate* that I need to put the dirty laundry in the washing machine. I know, however, that the washing machine is already full and running. It's *Obvious* what needs to happen with a basket full of dirty laundry but it isn't *Immediate*; so, the answer is *Nothing*.

"Dad, I feel depressed."

This is like this. (My child is telling me something important.)

1. *Who is experiencing this? I* (experience my child telling me something important.)

2. *When am I experiencing this? Now* (my child is telling me something important now.)

3. *What does Now need from me?* Nothing or Something

What is *Obvious* and *Immediate*? (listen to my child)

Can you see how the third question is now full of infinite possibilities? I'm not limited by the past story and I'm not required to do anything. I am absolutely free to take any action, I'm absolutely free to take no action.

Also, if the answer is Something, you only have to do that one Something and then the situation has changed. Because the situation changed, you can use The Recipe with the new situation. This naturally turns even the most complex and complicated problem into a simple situation that just needs your attention, step-by-step, all along the way.

Celebrate Good Times

The last step is *Celebrate!* If *Now* needs *Nothing*, *Celebrate!* If *Now* needs *Something*, attend to it and then *Celebrate!* This doesn't mean throwing a party every time you start the dishwasher or brush your teeth. It means, enjoy life, *Celebrate!*, when there is *Nothing* needed and *Celebrate!*, enjoy life, when you finish attending to Something. It means ENJOY LIFE!

Let yourself enjoy the peace of *Nothing* and the accomplishment of *Something*.

This is like this. (My child is telling me something important.)

1. *Who is experiencing this? I* (experience my child telling me something important.)

2. *When am I experiencing this? Now* (my child is telling me something important now.)

3. *What does Now need from me? Nothing* or *Something*

What is *Obvious* and *Immediate*? (listen to my child)

4. *Celebrate!* (enjoy the moment)

The Recipe!

That's it, that's The Recipe. Here's the whole thing written out for you. Write it out for yourself on a 3 x 5 card and stick it on the fridge.

<u>The Recipe</u>
This is like this.

1. Who is experiencing this? I
2. When am I experiencing this? Now
3. What does Now need from me?
   Nothing or Something
     Obvious and Immediate
4. Celebrate!

Now, don't believe me about The Recipe. Put your mind to work right now. Can you think of any situation where The Recipe won't work?

Take your time and think about it.

I use The Recipe every day with everything I do. I've never been able to find anything where it doesn't work or where it isn't effective. The only time it doesn't work or isn't effective is when I don't use it.

If you can't think of a single situation where The Recipe won't work, it sounds like you should use it in every situation.

At first, you'll have to remind yourself to use it all the time. Set a timer on your phone just like you did when you started practicing Kitchen Magic. Use The Recipe every time a problem appears, every time there's a decision to be made or every time the timer beeps. Use it for everything.

A Shopping List

Now you have The Recipe, but having it won't do you any good until you use it.

Having The Recipe and not using it is like making a cup of chai and never drinking it. Who does that?!

Sometimes you might have so many things on your plate that everything feels immediate. Everything needs your attention NOW! That's what it feels like but, that's not the reality of it.

The reality is, The Recipe still works, but you're like a kid in a candy store, you have too many options!

This is where a Shopping List comes in handy. A Shopping List is a list of five things that need your attention in the future. They might be an enormous project, like building a house. They might be something smaller, like planning a cross-country trip or spring cleanup or even dirty laundry.

Nothing is too big or too small to be on your Shopping List. The only thing to remember is that your Shopping List can only have five items on it. You're free to change what's on your Shopping List as often as needed. You're absolutely free to change it. It can only have five things on it.

How does the Shopping List work?

First, make a Shopping List. Then put it aside. It is not a to do list, it's a Shopping List.

Second, use The Recipe until nothing needs *Something* in the room where you are.

Third, once nothing needs *Something*, take a 5 to 20 minute break and do nothing. Relax and *Celebrate* for a moment.

Fourth, look at the first item on your Shopping List. Is there anything *Obvious* and *Immediate* about it?

- If you find something *Obvious* and *Immediate*, that's the next *Something*. Get started on it. When you finish that item, take a break, *Celebrate*, and then start over with your Shopping List.
- If you find something *Obvious* but not *Immediate*, make a note of it. Move onto the next item on your Shopping List.
- Continue this until you go through the Shopping List from start to finish.
- When you reach the end of the Shopping List, it's time to reapply The Recipe to the room.

Remember, you can apply The Recipe to anything. Your Shopping List is just a different application of The Recipe.

Also, don't worry if this seems slightly confusing or overwhelming. In just a moment, I'll walk you through using The Recipe and a Shopping List step by step. You'll discover for yourself how ridiculously simple they are. You're also beginning to see how powerful The Recipe and Shopping List are together.

Action! Make a Shopping List

Let's put this all together in the most effective way.

First, make a Shopping List. These are five tasks or projects that need your attention. Long-term projects and the things you try to avoid belong on your Shopping List.

Grab a piece of paper and a pen or pencil or grab your favorite electronic device for making lists. List out all the projects you have. Then list out all the things you prefer to avoid that still need your attention. List them *all* out.

Now you have a Laundry List. You can use the Laundry List to make a Shopping List. Identify the top five most difficult items on your Laundry List. That's your Shopping List.

Why start with the most difficult items? Because turning the most difficult items into simple situations using The Recipe first does two things. One, it gives you immediate proof that The Recipe works even with the most difficult things. Two, everything else is even easier.

If you haven't started yet, make a Laundry List now and use it to make your Shopping List.

Once you have the Shopping List, I suggest putting it on the fridge or fold it up and put it in your pocket. If it's on your phone or other electronic device, make sure you use one that you can easily carry with you.

The Shopping List must be easy to find and use. Make it as Obvious and Immediate as possible. It's also helpful if your Laundry List is easy to find.

Now that you have a Laundry List and a Shopping List, just write a quick note here in the conversation about any thoughts you have around this. Do you feel excited or skeptical? Does it make sense? Does it feel amazing?

Here or in your journal, write a few words about what you're thinking and feeling around making your Laundry List, Shopping List and using The Recipe.

Room Sweep

Now it's time to make a Room Sweep. What's that? I'll explain it by guiding you through it.

Do not move. Stay exactly where you are.

In a moment, turn your head all the way to the left and slowly sweep your eyes through the room, all the way around to the right. As your eyes travel from left to right, notice if anything needs your attention.

The moment you find something that needs your attention, stop. It's time for The Recipe. No matter how insignificant it is, notice that there's a slight experience of "*This should not be like this.*" That's often how you know that *something* that needs your attention.

Imagine your eyes land on a basket of clean clothes. A subtle sense of, "*This should not be like this. I should've put those away already.*" arises. Feel that for a moment.

Now that you've felt it for a moment, it's time to apply The Recipe.

The Recipe
This is like this.

1. Who is experiencing this? I
2. When am I experiencing this? Now
3. What does Now need from me?
   Nothing or Something
       Obvious and Immediate
4. Celebrate!

The clothes aren't put away. *This is like this.*

1. *Who is experiencing this? I am.*

2. *When am I experiencing this? Now.*

3. *What does Now need from me? Nothing* or *Something.* Clearly, the answer is *Something.* It's very *Obvious* what the basket of clean clothes needs. They need to be put away. It's *Obvious.* Can you immediately attend to it? If yes, then you have something that's *Obvious* and *Immediate.*

Put the clean clothes away.

4. *Celebrate!* Take a few minutes to enjoy Now.

After you *Celebrate*, start again. Sit in the same location and start the Room Sweep again. If you find something else that needs your attention, apply The Recipe.

What do you do if something is *Obvious* but not *Immediate*? Put it on the Laundry List. Once it's on the Laundry List, continue the Room Sweep.

Start your own Room Sweep now and when you finish it, which means your eyes went from the left side to the right side without finding anything that needs your attention, come back to the conversation.

[Do not continue the conversation until the Room Sweep is complete]

Now that the Room Sweep is complete, it's Break Time. You've been celebrating all along the way and now it's time to *Celebrate* even more! Give yourself 5 to 20 minutes to relax and enjoy a room empty of things that need your immediate attention.

Now that the Room Sweep and Break Time are finished, grab your Shopping List.

Start with the first item on the Shopping List and see if there is anything *Obvious* and *Immediate*. If you discover any resistance to what you find, apply The Recipe. If you find something that's *Obvious* but not *Immediate*, add it to your Laundry List and go on to the next item on the Shopping List.

Once you've gone through the Shopping List, you have a decision to make. You can either take the rest of the day off or move to another room and start another Room Sweep.

How do you know which one to do? If you're applying all of this at work, and the workday isn't over, then you might not want to take the rest of the day off. If you're applying this at home, you can just make that choice yourself. You could also apply The Recipe to that choice. That would be excellent practice using The Recipe.

There isn't one set approach that you have to take. There isn't one right way.

Using The Recipe

The Room Sweep uses The Recipe for the most mundane of things. Why? Those mundane things are easy. They're like going to the gym and lifting 5 pound weights.

You can't walk into the gym and start lifting 500 pounds on your first day. If you try, and you don't hurt yourself, you'll become so disappointed that you can't lift 500 pounds that you'll give up going to the gym.

The Room Sweep is like the 5 pound weights. You're learning the technique. You're also using The Recipe effectively. Using The Recipe effectively builds your confidence and trust in it and in your ability to use it effectively.

Life provides multiple opportunities, those things we call problems, to use The Recipe every day. If you only apply it to those things you think of as problems, it won't be very effective for you. If you apply it to everything, it will become extremely effective almost immediately.

The moment you notice garbage magic is happening and you're seeing problems, notice that the situation has the quality of garbage magic. "This should not be like this!" Use The Recipe to get out of the problem and into what's needed.

The Recipe

This is like this.

1. Who is experiencing this? I
2. When am I experiencing this? Now
3. What does Now need from me?
   Nothing or Something
       Obvious and Immediate
4. Celebrate!

You will forget to use it. That's human nature. The moment you recognize you forgot to use The Recipe, laugh at yourself for not using it and then USE IT!

From nice idea to reality

If you go through this part of the conversation, *Action!*, at least once a day for the next week, it will change your life forever. I know that's a bold statement. I also know that *Now* is perfect. That means you are perfectly prepared to change your life not by changing the problems and circumstances and environment of your life but by using The Recipe to change the way you interact with the life you live.

I also know that if you don't take that crazy leap, if you don't start using The Recipe *Now*, that everything we have talked about will stay a nice idea that never benefits you.

If you're at this point in the conversation and have done what I asked you to do, then you already know, firsthand, the effectiveness of The Recipe.

Good job!

If you haven't followed through, that's OK, *Now* is perfect. Just go back to the start of this part of the conversation and follow through. It's really that simple.

You deserve the benefits of The Recipe in your life. USE IT!

Write about it!

5

BONUS

Trauma: It Happened When I Was . . . .

I've already mentioned this, but I need to add this to our conversation, so it's very clear.

The Recipe is most easily applied to laundry baskets full of clean clothes. It can apply to workplace situations, family issues and all kinds of relationships. It can apply to emotional situations, including but not limited to the effects of anxiety, depression and even trauma.

I need to say one thing about trauma specifically: What happened when you were six years old doesn't matter. I know that can sound harsh, but I'm not saying something traumatic didn't happen to you. It means that even if you were in a traumatic experience yesterday, what happened yesterday doesn't matter. The details of what happened, the event itself, are in the unchangeable past. You can't do anything about the past, so that part doesn't matter.

All that does matter is what's happening *Now*. Two days ago my son had a panic attack because *Now* reminded him of when he experienced a scary situation as a child 20 years ago. What happened 20 years ago cannot be changed, ever. It's inaccessible and unchangeable. All that mattered was what he was experiencing *Now*.

What you are experiencing *Now* has a reality. You can feel it. Yes, you might even feel the leftovers from that traumatic event of the past, but you are feeling the leftovers *Now*.

Focus on what you experience *Now* because nothing else matters. The *past* doesn't matter because you can't do anything with it. *Now* matters because you can do *everything* with it.

You can't heal the past, it is unchangeable. You can't do anything with the past. The past doesn't matter.

You can't apply The Recipe to the past.

You *can* apply The Recipe to what's happening *Now*. *Now* is the only time you can use The Recipe. That's the reason for step #2 "**When am I experiencing this? Now**".

This is extremely important to understand. Whatever happened in the past, whether it was 50 years ago or five minutes ago, it doesn't matter. The only thing that matters are any aftereffects happening *Now*.

The more you apply The Recipe to those aftereffects, the less power they have. Soon, they have no power. If the past no longer has the power to affect the present, is it still a problem? No. That's why the past, no matter how terrible it may have been, doesn't matter.

Cooking For Others Is Not Possible

With great power comes great temptation. The Recipe is exactly like that. It's immensely powerful. It does have limitations. Some people can use The Recipe all their lives without bumping up against those limitations, and that's great. Most people, however, eventually find the limitations.

The first limitation people encounter arises when they try to use it to cook for someone else. You can't use The Recipe for anyone but yourself.

Let me repeat that and listen very carefully. You cannot use The Recipe to cook for other people. I, Ramdas, cannot use The Recipe to cook for other people, including you.

It is not possible.

Who is experiencing this? I am.

Let go of any ideas about cooking for other people. Give them The Recipe and let them cook for themselves.

Naturally, you have experience using The Recipe now; so, if someone has questions about using The Recipe, you likely have answers from your own experience. You likely have very helpful answers from your own experience. Report what you've experienced, but don't make the mistake of trying to cook for someone else. Don't do it, not even if they ask you to. It doesn't work.

The Unknown Future

The second limitation is The Unknown Future. It's difficult to use The Recipe to plan for the future. The Recipe focuses on *Now* and *Now* is not the future. It's also not very useful for the Unknown. If it's not *Here* and *Now*, The Recipe is not very helpful.

There is a Map that helps chart a course into The Unknown Future, but that's another conversation entirely.

6

INSPIRATION

The Source of The Recipe: I Can't Believe It's Not . . . .

So, where does The Recipe come from? How did I create such a simple technique that has so much power that it effortlessly turns any problem, no matter how complex, into a simple set of situations?

I didn't create it. It's been around for thousands of years. I can't even claim that I put it into easy-to-use steps. It really cooked that part up itself.

The Recipe is Yoga. This whole conversation has been Yoga. Well, that's not entirely true, let me explain.

Most people think Yoga is yoga postures. Yoga postures are not Yoga. Yoga postures are a place to experience Yoga.

Just like yoga postures are not Yoga, The Recipe is not Yoga. The Recipe is a place to experience Yoga.

So, what's Yoga? Yoga is a philosophy, a way of living life that reveals who you are. The Recipe reveals that. Who are you? *I.*

What's the benefit of knowing who you are and using this philosophy called Yoga to live life? Life starts to work for you. It's about living life with ease, no matter what's in front of you. It's about living life without fear. That's the purpose of Yoga.

That's the purpose of The Recipe: living life without fear. Living life, no matter how difficult, with ease and letting life work for you.

You've known this all along, even if you don't remember it, because I said it when we first started talking. I said, *"This is all about living life with greater ease, even when life isn't easy."*

When you know you can apply The Recipe to any problem —no matter how big, no matter how complicated—and turn it into a simple situation that just needs your attention. When you know that, what is there to be afraid of? With nothing to fear, you live life without struggle. You live life with ease.

Don't go hunting for things to be afraid of. Your mind will dream up all sorts of things right now if you let it. Just ask yourself, feel it, is there any situation in your life stronger than The Recipe? The Recipe transforms that scariest problem into simple circumstances and situations. What is there to be afraid of?

How can I be so sure The Recipe works in all situations? Lab work, lots of lab work.

Lab Work

It started with me. I realized something changed. I'll tell you about that in a minute, but when I recognized something changed, I started to investigate why it had changed.

After I started investigating, I became a mad scientist. I started to experiment with what I discovered using my students' experiences. These were my students in community yoga classes, in private sessions and in residential recovery centers. And just a quick disclaimer, everyone I worked with was a willing participant.

All the experiments returned positive results. At the very least, everyone found greater relaxation and relief from what they were experiencing. That alone is beneficial, but it's only temporary.

For 14 years, I've examined what I have experienced and what my students have experienced. I've studied ancient texts and with modern masters. What I extracted out of all of this lived experience is now The Recipe.

The Recipe has the potential to become spontaneous and automatic. All you have to do is practice it, use it.

You practice something so it becomes second nature, spontaneous and automatic. When something becomes **SP**ontaneous and **A**utomatic, it becomes SPA-like. (Yes, a terrible dad joke.) But it's true. When something becomes second nature to you and you've worked and practiced so long for that to be the case, it becomes an effortless, automatic, spontaneous experience. An **E**ffortless, **A**utomatic, **S**pontaneous **E**xperience is EASE.

During our conversation, I received a text from a middle-aged man who said, "The only reason I'm alive right now is I know this is like this. I keep asking: what does it need from me?" When I called him later, he literally said it had saved his life.

The teachings that have become The Recipe saved my life too.

Company is Stronger: Ramdas

I introduced myself earlier. It would've been impolite if I hadn't.

As of today, I've lived more than 50 years on this planet. For 30 of those years, I've been married to my wonderful wife, Shanna. We have four children, one son-in-law and two grandsons.

I survived depression for 30 years. That depression started when I was only 8 years old. When I was 10 years old, I tried to hang myself so I could end the sadness. Clearly, that didn't work, nor did the other two attempts. I'm thrilled that I failed.

What ended that depression? It wasn't yoga. I had been practicing yoga for seven years and that just made things much more intense. It was only when I began to understand *Yoga* and to live through that understanding that the depression ended. But that's an entire story by itself.

In the 14 years that I have lived depression free, I've continually been refining how to give to others what I have received. How to do it in a way the word yoga doesn't need to be used because that word scares some people off.

The result is The Recipe and this conversation.

But who am I really? "Hey look. He's just this guy, ya know?" and *I AM I.*

I hope you'll also think of me as your chai buddy.

Please indulge me as I tell you a little about some influential people, how they saved my life and contributed to the creation of The Recipe.

Chandrakant

Chandrakant is my first mentor, friend and guru-brother.

His journey took a pivotal turn when he decided to give life 15 minutes. In those 15 minutes, life would either provide him away to reach his guru or he would find a way out of life. Two minutes later, a fellow in a truck picked up the hitchhiking Chandrakant.

The man driving the truck was headed out of town to rescue his girlfriend from some crazy yoga group. Chandrakant was trying to get to that same crazy yoga group.

I've watched Chandrakant over the years like a hawk. He refuses to be fooled by his own beliefs. He verifies everything. One of the first things he said to me was, "Do not believe a single word I say." Sound familiar?

He's the one who taught me the little exercise you experienced when I asked, "Who are you?"

He was our guru's housekeeper and cook for many, many years and now he's one of the senior most teachers in our lineage because, as he puts it, "I'm the last one standing."

He's the last one standing because he would never allow himself to just believe something.

I love him dearly, and our conversation has been seasoned with the wisdom and understanding that he shared with me and I have now shared with you.

Gurudev

My guru is Yogi Amrit Desai. I call him Gurudev. He calls me Ramdas.

Gurudev turned 90 years old, October 16th, 2022. What a celebration we had!

At age 15, he met his guru, Swami Kripalvanandji or Bapuji, and fell in love with him. Gurudev learned everything he could from Bapuji.

In 1960, Gurudev came to America. He went to school and received a bachelor of fine arts degree. He's also an amazing artist and his paintings have won many awards. Over the years, he's written multiple books, which have also won multiple awards. He founded multiple yoga centers.

He loved his wife to the day she died and when we found a small picture of her a few days ago, he said to me, "There's my favorite." He loves his three children, their spouses and his grandchildren unconditionally.

But none of that is his life's work.

His life's work began at 15 when he met Bapuji. It took a major turn in 1970 when he had an awakening experience. He had taught yoga for years already, but in that moment;

he realized he knew nothing about Yoga and simultaneously he learned everything about Yoga.

If you've ever had an "Aha!" moment, you've had a small version of that same awakening.

His life's work is to give to others what they need to transform their own lives. He's given that to me, as well as countless others. What he gave me saved my life. It saved my marriage and my family. I've taken what he gave me and extracted out of it The Recipe.

The Recipe is only the beginning. It's the most simplified version of all that Gurudev teaches. Still, it's immensely powerful. Just using it will transform your life. Just know, there's more where it came from when you want it.

Bapuji

Gurudev's guru is Swami Kripalvanandji, or Bapuji, as we call him. He was born in 1913. He died in 1981.

He described himself as a pilgrim on the path of love.

At 19, he decided to end his life by throwing himself in front of the train at midnight. All that day, he sat in his favorite temple crying tears of anguish. A little sadhu, a holy man of India, walked into the temple and offered his devotion at the altar.

As he walked out, this sadhu tapped the 19-year-old on the shoulder and said, "Come outside with me."

"You're planning suicide," he said, "do not do it." Bapuji denied this, and the old man described the young boy's plans. He had told no one. How did the old man know? The old man invited him to come to his home the next day.

The young boy did not throw himself in front of the train that night. Instead, he went to the home of the sadhu, Dadaji, the next day. He stayed there for 16 months, learning at the feet of his guru.

Have you noticed how many times suicide, the greatest of desperations, has appeared among the teachers of this lineage? Bapuji, Chandrakant, myself. All of us let go of that greatest desperation and found immense joy in life.

Gurudev didn't face suicide, from what I know, but he did face life literally taking everything away from him. He faced circumstances that could have become that greatest desperation.

Why didn't it?

It was because he was already living and embodying, to his very best, the teachings of Yoga. That protected him from falling into the darkness that leads to the thoughts of suicide. Instead, because he was living a life of Yoga, he used that circumstance, that situation, to deepen his own practice and to be filled even more with love and joy.

Peer Pressure

It's absolutely possible to use The Recipe just based on our conversation. You have absolutely everything you need to be successful with The Recipe.

It's also true that peer pressure makes everything easier. We usually think of peer pressure in a negative light. The usual example is a teenager doing something stupid because of peer pressure. The peer pressure made doing the stupid thing easier.

When you realize peer pressure makes everything easier, you can use it to your advantage. Gurudev and Bapuji both put it this way: Company is stronger than willpower.

Having the support of community, company or peers, makes your efforts more effective. Peer pressure makes everything easier.

If you visit *RamdasWrites.com/TheRecipe*, you'll find that there are multiple opportunities for online community through social media. Company is stronger than willpower and peer pressure makes everything easier.

Attention follows energy.

The main mechanic behind The Recipe is that energy follows attention. That means whatever you put your attention on gets bigger.

If you focus your attention on garbage magic, the garbage gets bigger. The purpose of the first line of The Recipe, *"This is like this."* is to interrupt the flow of energy headed toward garbage magic by shifting attention to reality. The reality is, *"This is like this."*

The steps of The Recipe focus your attention and energy in a productive way.

This takes some effort. The Recipe is all about living life with ease. It's not about the easy life because life is not always easy, but you can live through those difficult times with ease.

This is only the first step in this philosophy of life called Yoga. At some point, the question naturally arises, "What's next? I'm no longer controlled by the situations of life I used to think of as problems. What's next? I've moved from reacting to life to responding to life. How can I live in harmony with life? What's next?"

The answer is "Live a life of YES." That answer is also much larger than this conversation. We'll have another conversation soon.

Now, go and use The Recipe.

7

SUPPORT

Kitchen Aids: How To Use the Kitchen Aids

T hank you for having this conversation with me, for reading this book.

This section of the book, Kitchen Aids, contains some simple yogic techniques, some that you've already experienced, to support your use of The Recipe.

There are two things to extract from this section and from experiencing these techniques: the first is to recognize and experience a quiet mind. The Recipe has always been available to you. It probably seems obvious now, but it wasn't available previously because the mind was too loud, too noisy, too busy.

These techniques will help you become familiar with a quiet mind. They're also great for stress relief, so use them for that purpose too!

The second thing to extract is the sense of ease or relaxation that comes with them. Becoming familiar with this sense of ease will help you recognize when you're using The Recipe most effectively. When you're using The Recipe effectively, you'll spontaneously experience a similar sense of ease.

Don't believe me, try it out.

Remember, you can visit *RamdasWrites.com/TheRecipe* for a recording of me guiding all the following *Investigations*.

The Scripts

[*Remember, if you're using these scripts to create a private recording or you're using them to guide someone through these investigations, do not read the text between the brackets.*]

A Short Breather (Hamsa Breath)

Sit comfortably with the eyes closed.

If possible, breathe in and out through the nose.

Feel the movement of the chest and belly with each inhale and exhale.

[Pause 3—5 breaths]

On the next inhale, feel the breath flow in through the nostrils.

Follow the sensation of that inhale into the body to where it seems to stop.

Does it stop in the throat, or in the upper chest, or down into the middle chest?

It doesn't matter where the inhale stops.

Follow the sensation of the inhale to where it stops in the body.

Now follow the exhale.

Follow the sensation of the exhale out to about 6 inches in front of the face.

Inhale from that point, 6 inches in front of the face.

Follow the inhale to where it stops in the body.

Exhale, follow the breath out to 6 inches in front of the face.

[Pause 3—5 breaths]

Inhale, follow the breath to where it stops in the body.

Notice, there's a slight pause or hesitation before the exhale naturally begins again.

Follow the breath out to 6 inches in front of the face.

Notice, there's a slight pause or hesitation before the inhale naturally begins.

Focus on these pauses.

Inhale, pause.

Exhale, pause.

[Pause 3—5 breaths]

Notice that as you focus on the pauses, they become just a little longer, a little softer.

[Pause 3—5 breaths]

On the next inhale, listen and feel for the sound, "Hah" but don't actually make the sound.

Just listen and feel for the sound, "Hah" as you inhale.

On the next exhale, listen and feel for the sound, "Sah" but don't actually make the sound.

Just listen and feel for the sound, "Sah" as you exhale.

[Pause 2—3 breaths]

Inhale. Listen and feel for the sound, "Hah", then listen and feel for the sound "mmm" as you feel the pause where the breath stops inside the body.

The inhaling breath now has the silent sound and feel of "Hahmmm."

The exhaling breath has the silent sound and feel of "Sah."

Hahmmm-Sah. Hahmmm-Sah.

Continue with this Hamsa Breath until I ask you to stop.

[Pause 5—15 breaths]

Now let the breath return to its own natural rhythm,

And notice the effect of this short breather.

Notice how relaxed the body is.

Notice how soft the breath is.

Notice how quiet the mind is.

[Pause 3—5 breaths]

On the next inhale, let the inhale draw your attention out to the fingers and toes.

As you feel the fingers and toes, allow them to begin to move.

As the fingers and toes begin to move, allow them to begin moving the hands and feet.

As the hands and feet begin to move, allow them to move the arms and legs until the whole body begins gently moving and stretching.

Once you feel you're totally back in the body, take a moment to review what you noticed.

On rare occasions, some people feel a little agitated or anxious after this *Investigation*. If that happened for you, you did nothing wrong. Anxiety is a coping mechanism that keeps the mind busy and noisy in a belief that the noisy thoughts somehow keep you safe. This *Investigation* quiets the mind, and that sometimes activates anxiety's early warning systems.

If that happened for you, come back to this *Investigation* once a day for the next three days. You'll be surprised by how quickly what you experience in this *Investigation* changes.

Use this space or a journal to describe your experience.

EXTRA SPACE

Slow Motion Energy

Rest the hands on the knees or thighs with the palms facing up. In a moment, I'll ask you to use your imagination to visualize breathing in and out through different parts of the body; so, let the eyes close and feel the breath gently flowing in and out through the nose.

Long, slow inhales.

Slow, soft exhales.

[Pause 3 breaths]

On the inhale, follow the breath in to where it feels like the inhale stops inside the body.

Notice the familiar pause.

On the exhale, follow the breath out to about 6 inches in front of the face.

Again, notice the familiar pause.

[Pause 3 to 5 breaths]

Now, imagine there's a small opening in the belly just above the navel.

Inhale, feel the belly expand and the chest rise.

Exhale. Visualize and feel the breath flow down and out through the opening in the belly.

Inhale through the nose and exhale down and out through the belly.

Inhale nose, exhale belly.

[Pause 3 breaths]

As you exhale through the belly, imagine that you can now also inhale through the belly.

Inhale belly. Exhale belly.

Imagine the sensations you would feel around the opening at the belly as you breathe in and out through the belly.

Imagine those sensations so clearly you can feel them as you breathe in and out through the belly.

If you're not sure that you're feeling any sensations around the opening at the belly, simply take one or two fingers and touch where you've imagined the opening at the belly.

Make a little circular motion with the fingers.

Feel the sensations at the belly and then let the hand return to the knee or thigh.

Imagine and feel breath flowing in and out through the sensations at the belly.

[Pause 3 breaths]

As you exhale through the belly, bring attention to the center of the chest.

Imagine a small opening at the center of the chest, about the level of the heart.

Inhale through the belly and as you exhale, feel the breath and sensation rise up along the spine to the heart center and exit through the small opening in the chest.

Inhale through the belly.

Exhale through the chest.

Immediately notice the sensations that show up around the opening at the center of the chest, as you breathe in through the belly and out through the center of the chest.

Inhale belly. Exhale chest.

[Pause 3–5 breaths]

On the next exhale through the chest, allow the opening at the belly to close.

Inhale through the chest and exhale through the chest.

The breathing pattern now is: inhale chest and exhale chest.

Notice how the sensations subtly change as you inhale through the chest and exhale through the chest.

[Pause 3–5 breaths]

As you exhale through the chest, shift attention to the palms and imagine an opening, one in the center of each palm.

Inhale through the chest and as you exhale, feel the breath rise up to the shoulders, stream down the arms and exit the openings, one in the palm of each hand.

The breathing pattern now is: inhale chest, exhale palms.

Notice the sensations beginning to arise around the centers of the palms as you inhale through the chest and exhale through the palms.

[Pause 3–5 breaths]

As you exhale through the palms, allow the opening at the chest to close.

Inhale through the palms and exhale through the palms.

The breathing pattern now is: inhale palms and exhale palms.

Feel the sensations arising around the centers of the palms as you gently breathe in and out through the centers of the palms.

[Pause 3–5 breaths]

On the next inhale, allow the hands and forearms to begin slowly drifting up into the air.

As the hands and forearms come off the knees or thighs, allow them to rotate so the palms are facing one another.

Allow the hands to slowly move toward each other without allowing them to touch.

The moment you begin to feel sensation, perhaps a magnetic pressure, between the hands, let them stop.

When the hands stop, let them move away from each other until you feel a subtle pressure or sensation on the back of the hands and let them stop.

Allow the hands to slowly, gently move back and forth, allowing them to explore the sensations between the hands and on the backs of the hands.

[Pause 2 breaths]

If you're not sure whether you are feeling sensation between the hands or on the backs of the hands, let the movement stop.

Allow the hands to move very slowly back and forth, just an eighth of an inch, just a millimeter or two.

Move so slowly you can feel the subtle sensation on the palms and on the backs of the hands.

As soon as you feel that sensation, allow the movement to become larger, but still moving slowly.

[Pause 3–5 breaths]

Now shift attention and notice how quiet, how empty the mind is.

Shift attention back to the sensation in the hands as they move back and forth.

On the next exhale, allow the hands to drift slowly back down to knees or thighs.

Again, shift attention to the mind and notice how quiet, how empty it is.

As you exhale, allow the openings in the palms to close.

Inhale through the nose, exhale through the nose and open the eyes.

Open your eyes.

Notice how relaxed the body is.

Notice how soft breath is.

Notice how silent the mind is.

Rest in this silence and stillness for a while.

Space to describe your experience either here or in your journal.

MORE SPACE

Breathe Some More! Bowing Breath & Third Key

Sit comfortably either seated on the heels or with the legs extended straight out in front of you.

You can also simply sit comfortably in a chair.

Let the eyes close and focus on the movement of breath.

Long, slow inhale. Slow, soft exhale.

[Pause]

On the next inhale, gently extend up the spine and out the crown of the head.

As you exhale, gently drop the chin down toward the chest.

Feel the stretch along the back of the neck.

Feel that stretch continuing down the spine.

On the inhale, allow the chin to slowly rise up towards the ceiling.

Lift the chin, lift the chest and lean back slightly. Do not struggle or strain.

On the exhale, allow the chin to drop down toward the chest.

On the inhale, lift the chin, lift the chest, lean back slightly.

Continue this gentle movement coordinated with inhale and exhale at your own rhythm and pace.

[Pause 3-5 breaths]

On the next exhale, begin to hinge at the hips, extending the torso forward and down.

On the inhale, slowly rise back up, lift the chin, lift the chest and lean back slightly.

Continue this bowing breath, coordinating movement with breath at your own rhythm and pace.

[Pause 3–5 breaths]

On the next exhale, as the torso extends forward and down, notice there's a slight pause at the end of the exhale before the inhale begins.

At the end of the inhale, notice there is another slight pause.

Continue this bowing breath, noticing the pause at the end of the exhale and at the end of the inhale.

[Pause 3–5 breaths]

Notice how the pauses naturally become longer, softer.

[Pause 3–5 breaths]

The next time the body is in the upright position, allow the body to remain upright and allow the breath to return to its own natural rhythm.

Let the hands rest on the knees or thighs, palms up.

Bring attention to the center of the chest and feel the subtle movement of the chest with each inhale and exhale.

Imagine, visualize, and feel that you can breathe directly in and out through the center of the chest.

Feel the sensations beginning to arise around the center of the chest as you breathe in and out through the center of the chest.

[Pause 2–3 breaths]

As you exhale through the chest, bring attention to the centers of the palms.

Inhale through the chest and as you exhale, feel the breath rise up to the shoulders, stream down the arms and exit the centers of the palms.

Inhale chest and exhale palms.

[Pause 3–5 breaths]

As you exhale through the palms, imagine now that you can also inhale through the palms.

Inhale palms. Exhale palms.

Feel the sensations beginning to pool in the palms.

On the next inhale, allow the hands to rise off the knees or thighs until the arms are parallel to the floor. Allow the hands and forearms to rotate until the palms face one another.

Allow the hands to begin moving toward each other without touching.

As soon as you begin to feel sensation between the hands, let the movement stop.

Allow the hands to begin moving away from each other and as soon as you feel sensation on the back of the hands, let them stop.

Allow the hands to begin moving toward one another again.

Allow the hands to gently move back and forth, exploring the sensation between the hands and on the backs of the hands.

If you aren't quite sure that you're feeling sensation between the palms or on the backs of the hands, let the movement stop.

Allow the hands to move back-and-forth just an 1/8th of an inch or a millimeter or two until you begin to feel sensation between the hands and on the backs of the hands.

Allow the movements to become larger, the hands exploring the sensations between the palms backs of the hands.

[Pause 3–5 breaths]

Allow the hands and forearms to rotate until the palms are facing upward, towards the ceiling.

Let the hands move very slightly up and down.

Begin to feel the weight of the sensations in the palms.

Feel the heaviness of those sensations as they pool in the palms.

Feel that heaviness spreading along the forearms.

Sense the subtle ache in the arms as you feel the weight of this sensation.

Now give the hands, forearms, upper arms and shoulders the complete freedom to move in whatever way is needed to release the subtle tension found in the arms and shoulders.

Feel the arms, the shoulders and even the whole upper body moving effortlessly, spontaneously, to release any tensions in the upper body.

Notice the movements are happening without your direction, the body spontaneously and effortlessly responding to what is present without your guidance.

Attention is following energy.

[Pause 3–5 breaths]

Allow the body to return to a comfortable, upright position.

Space to describe your experience here or in a journal.

Integrative Relaxation

[Integrative Relaxation or Yoga Nidra is a sleep based guided meditation. It is usually practiced lying on the back. Feel free to place pillows under your knees and feet to relieve any tension in the low back. You may also want a little pillow and blanket. It's common to feel a little chilly during this meditation because it resets stress levels and allows blood pressure to drop.]

Lie down, be comfortable.

You can also experience Yoga Nidra while seated in a chair.

Close the eyes and allow attention to turn inward.

Bring attention to the breath.

Feel the body beginning to relax with each progressive exhalation.

Listen and feel the vibrations of the sounds in the room.

Focus on the most noticeable sound. Feel it.

[Pause briefly]

Now bring attention to a softer sound, perhaps the sound of your own breath.

Listen and feel the vibrations of this new, softer sound.

[Pause briefly]

Notice how the sound and sensation of the first sound moves into the background.

Now focus on the sound and vibration of the soft sound of your own breath.

Feel and hear each inhale and exhale.

[Pause 3–5 breaths]

Focus on the silence and stillness between each inhale and exhale.

Sense sound and sensation dissolving into that silence.

Merge into that silent space.

[Pause 3–5 breaths]

Be still.

Let go of all thoughts, worry, and tension.

Give yourself fully to a higher power. Relax, trust and let go . . . .

Breathe in fully and exhale with a deep sigh . . . .

And again, breathe in fully and exhale with a deep sigh . . . .

And let go even more . . . .

Feel a deep sense of contentment and peace in your heart.

Repeat these words silently in the mind three times,

"I am at peace with what is as it is. This is like this."

[Pause 3–5 breaths]

Maintaining this inner awareness, gently bring the palms together.

Create some heat in the hands by rubbing the palms together.

When the hands feel very warm, place the fingertips on the eyelids.

Cup the heels of the hands underneath the jaw.

The entire surface of the palms touching the face.

Feel the transfer of energy in the form of heat coming from the hands into the skin and muscles of the face.

Allow the fingertips to gently massage the eyelids and eyes.

[Brief pause]

Allow the fingertips to slide up into the eyebrows, massaging the eyebrows and the temples.

Massage the bridge of the nose and the orbit of the eye sockets.

[Brief pause]

Now give complete freedom to the fingers and hands to find any tension in the face—the forehead, the cheeks, the nose and lips, in front of or behind the ears—let the fingertips find the tension hidden beneath the skin boundary.

Feel the fingers gently tease the tension out of the muscles and connective tissues.

[Pause 5–10 breaths]

Now, place the entire surface of the palms on the face, fingertips on the eyelids.

Drop all expressions from the face.

Take a deep breath in and let go.

Take another deep breath in and let go even more.

[Brief pause]

Release the arms to the sides. You may cover the arms and place an eye pillow over the eyes if appropriate.

Feel the effects not only in the face but also in the fingers and palms.

Feel the sensations throughout the whole body.

[Pause 3–5 breaths]

Now bring attention back to the face.

With the next exhalation, allow all expressions to drop from the face.

Release the tiny muscles around the eyes and feel the eyeballs rest back in their sockets....

Release the tiny muscles around the mouth...

Feel the tongue rest in the mouth.

Feel the lower jaw gently opening, softening.

Allow the cheeks to soften towards the floor.

[Pause 3 breaths]

Feel the scalp resting on the skull.

Feel the neck softening, easing.

Be available to the entire range of sensations in the face and head.

[Pause 3–5 breaths]

Drop into a sense of the whole bodily presence.

Embrace this present moment's experience, undistorted by what you like or don't like.

This is like this.

Let go of what is going . . . let come that which is coming.

This is your connection to Source, the I AM that you are.

[Pause 3–5 breaths]

As we continue, remain as motionless as possible.

If you do need to move or make any adjustment, do so mindfully, so the movement becomes part of the meditation.

Then, return to stillness as soon as possible.

Remain awake. Stay in touch with the sound of my voice as you allow the entire body to respond to my words directly and non-mentally.

Feel any disturbances, whether external or internal, drawing attention more deeply inward.

[Pause 3 breaths]

In Yoga Nidra, you enter the subconscious energy body.

The energy body is felt in the form of sensations throughout the body.

Feel the sensations present in the body and let the mind merge and melt into those felt sensations, dropping into the energy body.

Let them carry you beyond the boundaries of the physical body and mind.

As you shift from thinking and doing to feeling and being.

[Pause 3 breaths]

Do absolutely nothing. Simply relax.

Bring all the attention to the center of the eyebrows toward the center of the forehead.

We call this area the Third Eye.

Drop into the deepest state of tranquility, stillness and peace at the Third Eye.

[Pause 3–5 breaths]

Now I will guide you through Hamsa breath.

On the next inhale, feel the breath flowing in through the nostrils.

Follow the sensation of that inhale into the body to the point where it seems to stop.

Now follow the exhale.

Follow the sensation of the exhale out to about 6 inches in front of the face.

Inhale from that point, 6 inches in front of the face.

Follow the inhale to where it stops in the body.

Exhale, follow the breath out to 6 inches in front of the face.

[Pause 3–5 breaths]

As you follow the breath in to where it stops, notice there's a slight pause or hesitation before the exhale naturally begins.

Follow the breath out to 6 inches in front of the face and notice there's a slight pause or hesitation before the inhale naturally begins.

Focus on the pauses.

Inhale, pause.

Exhale, pause.

[Pause 3–5 breaths]

Notice that as you focus on the pauses, they become just a little longer, a little softer.

[Pause 3–5 breaths]

On the next inhale, listen and feel for the sound, "Hah".

On the next exhale, listen and feel for the sound, "Sah".

[Pause 2–3 breaths]

Inhale and listen and feel for the sound, "Hah". Listen and feel the sound "mmm" in the pause where the breath stops inside the body.

The inhaling breath now has the silent sound and feel of "Hahmmm."

The exhaling breath has the silent sound and feel of "Sah."

Hahmmm-Sah. Hahmmm-Sah.

Continue this Hamsa breath until I ask you to stop

[Pause 5–15 breaths]

Let the breath return to its own natural rhythm.

Drop into the silent space where all doing stops.

Enter an effortless state of being.

[Pause 3–5 breaths]

Follow my direction as we move attention through the body.

There is no need to move or do anything.

Simply shift attention to each body part, as I name it.

Now shift all attention to the Third Eye, center of the eyebrows toward the center of the forehead.

Shift attention down to the pit of the throat, the right shoulder, the right elbow, right wrist.

Tip of the right thumb, right index finger, middle finger, ring finger, little finger.

Right wrist, right elbow, right shoulder.

Shift attention back to the pit of the throat and to the left shoulder, left elbow, left wrist.

Tip of the left thumb, left index finger, middle finger, ring finger, little finger.

Left wrist, left elbow, left shoulder.

Shift attention back to the pit of the throat and down to the heart center.

To the right side of the chest.

Heart center.

Left side of the chest.

Heart center.

Shift attention down to the navel point.

To the center of the pubic bone.

Now shift attention up to the navel point.

To the heart center.

Pit of the throat.

Third eye.

Allow attention to drop back 2 to 3 inches into that vast spaciousness behind the third eye.

Resting in this vastness, notice what comes into the field of awareness.

Thoughts, words, images, sensations.

Allow whatever arises to be present without judgment or comment.

"I am at peace with what is as it is. This is like this."

Simply witness it all as it floats by like clouds in the vastness of the sky.

[Pause 3–5 breaths]

Bring attention to a constricted or dense part of the body . . .

While you may not consciously recognize the cause of this feeling, the innate intelligence of the body knows how to resolve it.

Breathe into this area.

Feel each breath give the sensation room to move . . . . to expand . . . . to shrink . . . . to loosen . . . . to disperse.

[Pause 3–5 breaths]

Feel it dissolve and lighten.

Feel the body release what it no longer needs.

[Pause 3–5 breaths]

Feel the body's natural healing energy stream towards this area . . . . as if the area were attracting it like a magnet.

Watch this part of the body return to wholeness and vitality as the body's natural healing energy surrounds it.

With each inhalation, sense the body as more energy than density.

Until you feel the whole body as a pulsing, tingling field of energy.

[Pause 3–5 breaths]

Any emotions, thoughts, fears or doubts that may have contributed to the imbalance can now be released and resolved.

See and feel the whole body healed and whole.

[Pause 3–5 breaths]

Allow yourself to enter the deepest level of relaxation right now. Let go.

There is nothing to accomplish or achieve.

Dissolve and disappear into stillness.

Be open and empty.

Empty of all doing.

Empty of all past.

Empty of all future.

Merge into this space and be empty.

[Pause 3–5 breaths]

Sensations, thoughts, sounds and images, all floating by like clouds in a clear blue sky.

Let it all gather and dissipate.

Let it all come and go.

You are the space in which it is all happening.

[Pause 8–10 breaths]

Here, your intention and your affirmations are actualized and fulfilled with effortless ease.

Allow these words to once again fill the empty mind.

"I am at peace with what is as it is. This is like this."

Allow those words to repeat silently three times in the mind.

"I am at peace with what is as it is. This is like this."

Feel those words moving to the deepest levels of recognition with no hesitation.

Know that your higher self, I AM, recognizes, honors and accepts those words.

Have faith and trust that they have been heard and are being acted upon by a higher power of the source within you and there's no need for you to do anything about it.

[Pause 3–5 breaths]

Bring your attention back to the Third Eye and feel all the energies of the body from all meridians activated, purified and balanced.

Feel life force flowing freely.

Feel it healing the body and calming the mind.

Open your heart and feel content.

Just be.

[Pause 3–5 breaths]

Allow your entire self to respond spontaneously and effortlessly to what I say . . . .

I trust the path that has brought me to this moment.

I trust the path ahead to show the way.

"I am at peace with what is as it is. This is like this."

Establish yourself firmly in faith and trust to receive the grace, protection, and guidance of the higher self within you.

The more often you rest as this silent source, the easier it is to return here and the longer you can stay.

Feel the presence of your own spiritual guides. Feel them surrounding you and blessing you.

Accept their blessing and grace . . . embody it and spread it wherever you go.

You have prepared the foundation from where you can carry out interactions with life and all relationships using the integrative power of love and the light of the source within.

You are the emissary of that light and love.

Carry it everywhere you go and to everyone you meet.

If you have an area that you feel needs healing, physical, mental or emotional, allow this light and love to flow into that area now.

[Pause 3–5 breaths]

Now bring attention back to the breath.

Feel each inhale and each exhale.

On the next inhale, allow the inhale to draw attention out to the fingers and toes.

As you feel the fingers and toes, allow them to slowly begin to move.

As the fingers and toes begin to move, allow them to move the hands and feet.

And then the arms and legs.

Until eventually, the whole body begins to slowly move and stretch as if you were waking up from a very restful sleep.

Allow those movements to eventually guide the body to a comfortable seated position with the eyes closed.

Rest in this meditative experience for a while.

Use this space or a journal to describe your experience.

Learn More

All these techniques I learned either directly through years of training at the Amrit Yoga Institute or are directly based on what I have recognized and experienced through studying at the Amrit Yoga Institute.

You can have your own direct experience of this by connecting with the Amrit Yoga Institute either through the links at *RamdasWrites.com/TheRecipe* or you can browse to *AmritYoga.org* directly.

Chai Recipe

For the full chai recipe experience, please go to *Ramdas Writes.com/TheRecipe* and watch the video, "Chai Bhagwan!"

Ingredients

- Good quality loose tea. Assam black tea or loose peppermint tea are preferred.
- Chai masala
- Cardamom
- Milk
- Water
- Sweetener

Chai masala ingredients

- 4 parts ground ginger
- 3 parts ground black pepper
- 2 parts ground cinnamon
- 1 part ground cloves

If you use a teaspoon to measure, that's 4 teaspoons ground ginger, 3 teaspoons ground black pepper, etc.

Add all the masala ingredients to a container that you can securely close. Close the container and shake it vigorously. You now have chai masala.

Instructions

1. Fill the cup that you will drink the chai from half with water and half with milk. Pour the milk and water mixture into a saucepan.

2. Using a small teaspoon, not a measuring teaspoon, add one spoonful of loose tea to the saucepan.

3. Add approximately 1/4 of the same teaspoon each of chai masala end of cardamom to the saucepan.

4. Bring the mixture to a rolling boil, stirring constantly. Be very attentive, as it will try to boil over. As the chive foams, lift the saucepan off the heat and stir the bubbles back down. Return the pan to the heat and repeat two more times. This means the chai will foam up 3 times.

5. Pour the chai through a fine tea strainer and sweeten to taste.

6. "Go and have some tea." Enjoy the chai.

The instructions make one cup of chai. You can make as many cups as needed by simply increasing the amount used appropriately.

Visit *RamdasWrites.com/TheRecipe* and watch the video, "Chai Bhagwan!" to see me use this recipe to make 2 cups of chai.

Now, go and have some tea!

ABOUT THE AUTHOR

Ramdas Ormond has been a teacher and mentor for over 20 years. He has helped thousands of people from 21 countries on 6 continents find ease in their daily lives. His passion for teaching comes from his own journey to freedom after 30 years of depression.

For the last 8 years, Ramdas has focused on those in addiction recovery. He knew that if what he offered could help those in recovery, it could help anyone. He combined his own experience, the guidance of his mentors and his study of ancient teachings to create The Recipe.

You can find Ramdas on BlueSky and Facebook .

BlueSky: bsky.app/profile/ramdas.bsky.social

Facebook: facebook.com/RamdasWrites